Measuring Instructional Results

or Got A Match?

*How to find out if
your instructional objectives
have been achieved*

Revised Third Edition

Robert F. Mager

Mager Associates, Inc.
Carefree, AZ

Books by Robert F. Mager:
  Preparing Instructional Objectives, Revised Third Edition*
  Measuring Instructional Results, Revised Third Edition*
  Analyzing Performance Problems, Revised Third Edition*
    (with Peter Pipe)
  Goal Analysis, Revised Third Edition*
  How to Turn Learners On . . . without turning them off,
    Revised Third Edition*
  Making Instruction Work, Revised Second Edition*
  What Every Manager Should Know About Training,
    Second Edition
  Troubleshooting the Troubleshooting Course
  Life in The Pinball Machine, Second Edition
* Also sold as a six-volume set (The Mager Six-Pack)

Workshops by Robert F. Mager:
  Criterion-Referenced Instruction (with Peter Pipe)
  Instructional Module Development
  The Training Director Workshop

Requests for permission to make copies of any part of this
publication should be mailed to:
  Mager Associates, Inc.
  P.O. Box 2180
  Carefree, AZ 85377

ISBN: 9781622091416
ISBN: 9781622091454 (Six-Volume Set)

Printed in the United States of America.

Contents

Preface

Once upon a time, as the crow flies, the king of Hairmania decided to shave off his beard.

"It is an event that will bring attention and fame—not to mention tourists," he beamed. "Bring the Royal Barber."

"But sire," lamented his advisor, "there are none left in Hairmania. No one has been allowed to shave for a hundred years."

"Hairesy!" exploded the king. "No wonder we're so crowded. Sally ye forth, therefore, and find me the best in all the land."

Which he did. And when at last the most famous barber was found, he was sent to the Royal Three Committees for the Royal Testing.

"Tell us about the history of barbering," asked the first committee.

And he did.

"Tell us about the importance of barbering," asked the second committee.

And he did.

"Tell us what instruments you would use to shave the king," asked the third committee.

And he did.

Whereupon they draped his neck with their Medallion of Approval and led him before the king. Wasting no time, the barber prepared his tools and spread his cloth. But when he picked up his razor with a swirling flourish—he accidentally sliced a piece off the king's ear.

"Gadzooks!" cried the king. "You've cut off my royal ear!"

"Oops," chorused the nine voices of the Royal Three Committees.

"*Oops?*" astonished the king. "I ask for *skill* and you give me *oops?*"

"We're very, very sorry," apologized the Royal Three Committees. "We must have lost our heads."

"A capital idea," rejoiced the king, and sprang himself forth to make it decidedly so.

And ever since and forever more,
There hang nine heads on the Royal Door.
For this was the fate of the Committees Three . . .
May it never befall such as me . . . or thee.

And the moral of this fable is that:

HE WHO ASKS WRONG QUESTIONS MAY LOSE MORE THAN FACE

—RFM

Unlike the Committees Three, we would never think to measure barbering skill by asking about the history of barbering . . . would we? Neither would we weigh steam with a yardstick or evaluate music with a bathroom scale. Similarly, we shouldn't measure the results of our instruction with instruments (i.e., test items) that are inappropriate for the task at hand.

The Focus

There are any number of things that might be useful to know about the effects of one's instruction. For example:

- Did the students *like* the instruction?
- Would they recommend the instruction to others?
- Did the students experience obstacles to learning?
- Did the instruction do what it was supposed to do?
- Do the students use what they learned on the job, in their daily lives, or during subsequent courses?
- Can the instruction be delivered more smoothly, i.e., are there opportunities for improvement?

These and other questions are all legitimate subjects of inquiry. Only one, however, is the direct focus of this book— whether the instruction did what it was supposed to do. There is good reason for this emphasis. Until you know how well your instruction is doing what it is supposed to be doing, there is little reason to evaluate anything else. Why? Regardless of the eloquence of the instructor or the cleverness of the procedures used, instruction is of little value unless its objectives are achieved—unless students depart the instruction able to perform at least as well as the objectives require.

That's why the focus of this book is on learning how to find out whether instruction has accomplished its purpose. It's the most important thing to know about a piece of instruction.

This book is therefore designed to provide you with the basic tools through which to measure instructional success.

The Objective

Specifically, the objective of this book is this:

> Be able to discriminate (select, point to) test items that are appropriate (i.e., items that match the objective in performance and conditions) for testing the achievement of an instructional objective, when given (1) an objective, (2) one or more allegedly suitable test items, and (3) the Objective/Item Matching Checklist.

In short, this book is about how to find out whether your instruction has succeeded as you intended.

Robert F. Mager
Carefree, Arizona

What It's All About

1

Suppose you worked hard to achieve this objective handed you by the instructor on the first day of the course:

On a level paved street, be able to ride a unicycle one hundred yards without falling off.

Suppose you had strengthened your thighs with deep-knee bends and had practiced riding until you could mount and ride with relative ease for at least two hundred yards. And suppose that when testing time came around, your instructor asked you to get out pencil and paper and answer the following questions:

1. Define *unicycle.*

2. Write a short essay on the history of the unicycle.

3. Name at least six parts of the unicycle.

4. Describe your method of mounting a unicycle.

What would be your reaction? How would you feel if you had been told to learn one thing and were then tested on another? And how would the instructor ever find out whether the objective had been achieved?

Suppose the instructor "justifies" this situation to you with one or more of the following comments. How would (did) you feel?

"We don't have the facilities to give performance tests."

"We don't have enough unicycles to go around."

"This is an educational institution, not a training institution."

"It doesn't matter how well you can ride; if you don't know anything about the unicycle, you can't really appreciate it."

"I'm teaching for transfer."

"It's too easy to learn to ride a unicycle; I have to add some harder items so I can grade on a curve."

"If everybody learned to ride, I'd have to give everybody an A."

"I like to vary the type of items I use to make my tests interesting."

"I want my tests to be a learning situation."

"I'm teaching creativity and insight."

"I have to design my tests so they can be machine scored."

"Students should learn by discovery."

Regardless of the truth or falsity of the comments listed above, the fact remains that you *cannot* find out whether a person can ride a unicycle unless you or someone else watches that person ride one. In other words, you cannot find out if the objective is achieved unless you use test items that ask the student to do whatever the objective is about. If you use items that aren't "right" for an objective, not only will you *not* find out if your objective has been achieved, you may fool yourself into thinking it has. That can make a person feel pretty silly and unprofessional to students who know an irrelevant, unrealistic, unfair test item when they see one.

That's not so bad when an objective isn't very important, but when there are significant consequences for achieving or not achieving an objective, you'd better take appropriate steps to *find out* whether it has been achieved. If it matters whether the patient's temperature is less than 100 degrees, you'd better use a thermometer to measure temperature rather than a yardstick ... or a multiple-choice exam. If it matters whether a student pilot can react quickly and accurately in a stall emergency, then you'd better use a reaction-producing item rather than a thermometer ... or an essay. If it matters whether a student is able to read at least two hundred words per minute, then you'd better find out if that skill can be performed. You'll then be able to respond with more instruction when it can't or with applause when it can, rather than with merely a label (i.e., a grade).

The View From the Top

Unless they are talking about instruction, most people have no difficulty whatever in deciding how to measure results. Ask them how they would find out whether a cake is any good, and most will reply, "Taste it." It is unlikely that anyone would suggest that you should measure the characteristics of the cook or that you should evaluate the *process* of baking.

Similarly, if you asked people how they would find out whether someone could write an essay, they would have no trouble responding, "Well, I'd have them write an essay." It wouldn't even occur to them to respond, "Well, I'd ask the students to describe the characteristics of an essay," or, "I'd give the students an essay and ask them to edit it (or correct it, comment on it, etc.)."

Only when we enter the instructional world do we seem to have difficulty in making the connection between the accomplishment we want to measure and the means of measuring it; between what we want to know and what we should do to find it out.

Measuring the accomplishment of an objective isn't hard.

One merely has to prepare test items that ask students to demonstrate the performance called for by the objective, i.e., to demonstrate the point of the objective. In other words, one prepares items in which the performance and conditions match those of the objective to be assessed. In practice, it's only a little more difficult than the telling. (Those who have well-stated objectives derived from analyses may well wonder what the fuss is all about; they already follow this procedure as a matter of course.)

> **NOTE:** A performance will be judged according to the criteria stated in an objective, of course, but it isn't necessary to include those criteria in the test items. Why not? Often there are several criteria by which the performance will be judged and to include them in a test item would serve only to confuse the student. Also, when more than one item is used, the criteria by which the performance will be judged are applied collectively to all the items; it would make no sense to include criteria in each. It is usually enough for the item simply to tell the student what to do, as well as where and with what (or without what) to do it.

Obstacles

The difficulties experienced while writing items seldom are caused by an inability to craft suitable test items. Instead, they are caused by poorly written objectives. When people try to test the accomplishment of vaguely-written objectives, they find it impossible to decide what type of measuring instrument to use. And no wonder. If you're not clear about what you want to measure, it's not possible to decide intelligently how to measure it.

Another important obstacle to easy preparation of suitable test items arises from the tendency of instructors to consider the student fair game for almost any kind of test. This tendency somehow gives instructors a feeling of uneasiness when they construct test items strictly according to the objective. "These items don't cover enough ground," the feeling says. "These items are too easy," it tells them; and it makes them conveniently forget that the object is not to develop a variety of items that only half the students can master, but to prepare items that will reveal which students can perform as desired. And the feeling goes on to say, "Well, maybe students can perform as well or better than expected, but they won't really understand it unless . . ." and then urges instructors to add items having little or no relation to the objective. Finally, this funny feeling, in a last desperate bid for survival, says, "Well, maybe all the students have achieved the objective, but I need to add some harder items so I can spread them out on a curve."

I can help you avoid that feeling by describing the rationale for the procedure described in this book and by helping you develop skill in implementing that procedure. After all, people who know how to do something are more likely to do it than those who don't know how! And if they know why they are doing it, they may feel more at ease when following the more productive path.

> **NOTE:** The use of inappropriate test items is a widespread phenomenon and is a practice (malpractice?) most urgently in need of jettisoning. When we deceive students by teaching one thing and testing another, we lose and the students lose. Putting it more plainly, when we cheat students, they generally find a way to cheat back. Everyone associated with education and training need to know how to avoid that.

What's to Come

So that words won't get in our way, the next chapter will describe a few distinctions in terms. Following that, there will be discussion and practice in interpreting—decoding—the key characteristics of an objective. That will prepare us for discussion and practice in matching potentially useful test items to objectives.

Then, before practicing the entire skill, you can practice repairing some items to match the objectives they are supposed to be related to. Finally, a set of items is provided with which you can test your skill.

NOTE: Because the actual objectives we see and use vary considerably in the clarity with which they are stated, I will use similarly imperfect statements in the examples that follow. After all, we need to learn to handle the world as it is, rather than to practice only on well-stated objectives that you may seldom encounter.

2
Distinctions

Barriers to communication arise when words have different meanings to different people. To avoid this possibility, a few definitions and distinctions are in order. If we both use words in the same manner, they won't get in the way of our ideas.

Items and Tests

It is useful to be able to tell the difference between tests and test items. If you've ever spent much time in a school, you couldn't avoid either one, so this distinction may appear obvious. Then again, maybe not.

Item: A test item calls for a single response or set of responses to a single stimulus or stimulus pattern. It asks for one sample of a behavior. That performance may be simple, as when asking someone to write the answer to an addition problem, or it may be complex, as when asking someone to perform an appendectomy, analyze a problem, compose a sonata, fly a plane, or operate a computer.

Test: A test is an event during which someone is asked to demonstrate some aspect of his or her knowledge or skill. Though a test can consist of a single test item, a test generally consists of several items.

NOTE: Because of the uncomfortable emotional baggage often associated with the word "test," tests (especially in industry) are referred to as "skill checks" or "performance checks." These are especially appropriate terms in environments where the purpose of the exercise is to find out whether someone can now perform as desired, rather than to collect information on which to base a grade.

Measurement, Evaluation, and Grading

Measurement: The process of measurement determines the extent of some characteristic associated with an object or person. For example, when we determine the length of a room or the weight of an object, we are measuring.

Evaluation: The act of evaluation compares a measurement with a standard and passes judgment on the comparison. We are making evaluations when we say things like—it's too long, it's too hot, he's not motivated, she's too slow. To arrive at these evaluations we have noted the extent of some characteristic, compared it with some standard, and then passed judgment on the comparison.

When we then say things such as:

> "She passed."
> "He flunked."
> "She's not working up to her potential."
> "He's competent."

we are making *evaluations*. We have compared the results of the measurement with some standard (real or imagined, stable or floating, visible or invisible) and have made a judgment.

The difference between measurement and evaluation can be illustrated by this example:

Measurement: "These watermelons are three feet long."

Evaluation: "Wow!"

Or by this example:

Measurement: "This student can type 30 words per minute."

Evaluation: "That's too slow."

Grading: A grade is a label representing an evaluation. When you note that your cow has been stamped "U.S. Choice," you know that it has been given a grade. (What the cow had to do to deserve such a grade is another matter.)

Sometimes an evaluation is based on measurement and sometimes on guesses, intuition, expectation, or bias. Traditionally, a grade says something about how well a student has performed *in relation to his or her peers;* the student is very good, pretty good, about the same as, not as good as, or much poorer than those who happen to be his or her classmates. Also traditionally, the student is seldom informed of the precise basis for the grade.

Norm-Referenced and Criterion-Referenced Evaluations

Norm-referenced evaluation: When the performance of one student is compared with that of other students, and a judgment is made on the basis of that comparison, a norm-referenced evaluation has been made.

Thus, when we say that Student X is above average and that Student Y is below average, we are rank-ordering students on the basis of their performance *in reference to each other,* and therefore we are making a norm-referenced evaluation.

Grading on a curve is such an evaluation. So is the assignment of IQ.

For example, if we have five automobiles, and none of them runs, we might measure the extent of their defects and say "Automobile B 'doesn't run' the best. None of them goes at all, but B is the best of the non-goers." We've just made a norm-referenced evaluation. If we then said, "Give that car an A+," we would have assigned a grade on the basis of a norm-referenced evaluation.

> **Criterion-referenced evaluation:** When we make a judgment based on a comparison of a measurement with an objective standard, we make a criterion-referenced evaluation.

If, for example, we evaluate our automobiles and say "None of them runs," we've compared the state of each car with a standard that says, "It has to move to be acceptable," and judged that none meets this criterion. We have made a criterion-referenced evaluation.

Here's another example. Suppose students are expected to accomplish this objective:

> *Within three minutes, be able to solve fifty addition problems, without the use of a calculator.*

Suppose further that one student solves only 35 problems within the time allowed. There are two kinds of evaluation that can follow this measurement:

> **Norm-referenced:** "Gee, this performance is the best in the class. Give this student an A."

> **Criterion-referenced:** "Oops. This performance did not meet the criterion. Give this student more instruction and/or practice."

The Coffee-Pot Caper

The difference between the norm-referenced and criterion-referenced methods of evaluation was beautifully illustrated some years ago by an example that went like this: Imagine that an objective called for a student to be able to make a pot of coffee, when given all the necessary tools and equipment. A checklist of each of the steps in the process is prepared, and the student's performance is then scored on both a norm-referenced and a criterion-referenced basis. Note the difference between the two methods of scoring:

Checklist for Making a Pot of Coffee

	Norm-referenced Scoring	Criterion-referenced Scoring
Disconnects coffee pot	10	✓
Disassembles coffee pot	10	✓
Cleans components and pot	10	✓
Inspects components	10	✓
Fills pot with water	10	✓
Reassembles components	10	✓
Fills basket with coffee	0	✗
Reconnects coffee pot	10	✓
Sets dial on coffee pot	10	✓
Turns coffee pot on	10	✓
SCORE	90%	Not yet competent

Note that a norm-referenced approach would allow a student to accumulate a score of 90 percent, *even though the student failed to make a pot of coffee.* Using a criterion-referenced approach, on the other hand, the same student would receive a score of zero. By failing to accomplish the objective of being able to make a pot of coffee, the student must be judged to be "not yet competent." (Just last week I failed to put the little coffee pot under the spout of our espresso maker. I made coffee, all right, all over the kitchen counter . . . but my wife refused to give me 90% for my effort. Never mind what she did give me.)

Though there are some uses for norm-referenced evaluation, our attention will be focused on criterion-referenced evaluation. When we want to know *whether* an expectation (objective) or criterion has in fact been achieved, only criterion-referenced procedures are appropriate.

Criterion Items and Diagnostic Items

Criterion item: An item designed to help determine whether some criterion has or has not been achieved.

Diagnostic item: An item designed to reveal *why* a criterion was NOT achieved.

For example, if we want to find out if someone could bake a pie that met certain standards, we would use *criterion items* designed for that purpose. Simply, we would ask someone to bake a pie. If that person could do it, and if the pie met the standards set for it, we would say that the criterion had been met. He or she could bake a pie.

If, however, the pie did not get made at all, or if the finished pie oozed to the floor in a puddle, we would say that the would-be baker did not meet the criterion. When this is the case, we may want to know *why* the person did not meet the criterion—why the task wasn't performed as required. Items designed to find out *why* a criterion was *not* achieved are called *diagnostic* items.

The distinction is important. A test often contains both criterion items and diagnostic items; many contain *only* diagnostic items. If we don't know the difference between the two, we might decide *whether* a student has achieved a criterion by evaluating performance on a diagnostic item. Thus, if we want to know if a student can peel an orange, we should make that judgment on the basis of the criterion item, (e.g., "Peel that orange") rather than on the basis of diagnostic items (e.g., "Tell me *how* you would peel that orange," or "Is this an orange?" or "Whose team wears orange jerseys?").

The criterion item provides the proof of the pudding but doesn't help much with the recipe. A simple depiction of the uses of the two types of items is shown in the sketch below.

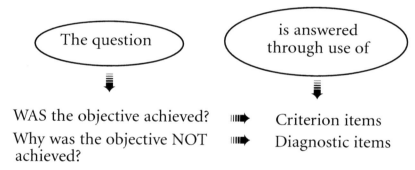

Although some criterion items can be useful for diagnostic purposes, the emphasis here is with using them to find out whether an objective has been accomplished. More on this in Chapter 6.

End-of-Course and On-the-Job Evaluations

Instructional effects can be assessed at several points along the instructional road. For example:

- **End-of-unit:** Criterion and diagnostic test items (skill checks) are used to determine whether a student has accomplished the objective of an instructional unit, so that remedial action can be taken when needed (e.g., additional practice).

- **End-of-course:** Skill checks (tests) are used to find out whether a student can be judged "competent" or "not yet competent." (It's risky to rely solely on end-of-course evaluations, of course, because there no longer is any time left to provide remedial help when a student is not yet competent.)

- **On-the-job:** Performance of the job incumbents (the former students) is assessed to determine whether they actually use what they were taught.

The end-of-unit and end-of-course evaluations tell us whether or not the instruction works; that is, whether it accomplished what it set out to accomplish. These are the assessments that will tell you whether a student can or cannot be judged competent.

On-the-job evaluations can tell you many things, but they cannot tell you whether the instruction was successful. Such evaluations, in fact, aren't *instructional* evaluations at all. If, for example, it is discovered on the job that people *don't know how* to do what they're supposed to do, it's possible that the instruction was somehow defective. However, when people don't perform their jobs right even though they know how to do so, it can't be legitimately inferred that the instruction was at fault. Why not? Too many variables interfere with such a conclusion; there are many reasons why people don't perform as expected, and a lack of know-how is only one of them. For example:

- They may not have the authority.
- They may not have the tools, space, equipment.

- They may not know what they're expected to do.
- They may get punished when they do it right.
- They may get rewarded for doing it wrong.

And more. When people are not performing on the job as expected, therefore, it is simply wrong to conclude that the training didn't work. In most situations, what isn't working right is management. Those interested in guaranteeing that their instruction does what it was designed to do will make sure their students can perform according to the objectives before they leave the instructional environment.

And Now?

Now that we've sorted out a few distinctions, it's time to plunge into the purpose of it all, that of selecting or writing test items that will measure accomplishment of an objective. To do that, though, we've got to be able to figure out what those objectives are saying. In other words, we need to be able to decode an objective so we can answer the eternal question, "Where's the beef?"

3
Decoding the Objective

Many procedures take longer to explain than to perform. Tying a shoelace, adding a column of numbers, and playing a sonata are examples. In each case, the skill can be performed faster than it can be explained—once the skill has been learned.

So it is with writing or selecting test items relevant to assessing an objective. The explaining takes longer than the doing, long enough to make the point worth mentioning. In practice, the drafting of a suitable test item will take but a minute or two. Only a small percentage of your items will take longer to think through and draft.

The Goal

We're seeking to be able to write or select items that will test achievement of an objective, that will help us decide whether our instruction actually accomplished what it was intended to accomplish. That means writing or selecting test items that ask students to:

(a) do what the objective asks them to be able to do,

(b) under the conditions described by the objective.

The objective wants students to be able to give speeches? Fine. We'll write a test item that asks them to give a speech. The objective wants the speech-giving to occur under water? OK, we'll add that condition to the test item. And that's that. Well, it would be that—if every objective were clear and contained the information you need to help you with your decision-making and if you didn't sometimes have to test under conditions different from those desired. Unfortunately, as the old song says, "It Ain't Necessarily So."

Why not? Simply because many objectives either don't tell you what you need to know, or they make you guess at what they really mean. Some "objectives" don't state a performance; those that do may still leave you wondering what the objective really is. Some will tell you how a performance should be measured without giving you a clue about what you're supposed to be measuring.[1]

If we didn't encounter so many objectives that don't do what they're supposed to do (some of which we write ourselves), we'd have no need to learn to decode an objective (that is, noting the presence or absence of key characteristics) and could go directly to the business of building measuring instruments to test their achievement. But because reality requires us to "Get real!" we need to take a little time out to make sure we can squeeze the information we need from an objective, even when it isn't cleanly stated.

What You Need to Know

To carry out the decoding procedure, you need to be able to recognize the difference between:

1. Performances and abstractions,

---

1. For more help in understanding objectives, read *Preparing Instructional Objectives, Third Edition*, R. F. Mager (The Center for Effective Performance, Atlanta, GA, 1997).

2. Main intents and indicator performances, and

3. Overt and covert performances.

Once you know how to make these distinctions, you'll not only be able to deal with well- and poorly-stated objectives, you'll find the decoding procedure a piece of cake. Of course, if you already can make these discriminations, it would be a waste of your time to have to read the sections that deal with them. Therefore, you have a choice. Turn to the page number shown beside the statement that best describes your decision.

I can already make these distinctions.   **Turn to page 33.**

I could use a quick review.   **Turn to page 20.**

Performances and Abstractions

Performances: Performances are things that people say and do. They sing, write papers, type, hit golf balls, solve problems, give speeches, make discriminations, and point to things. Performances are what objectives are about.

Abstractions: Sometimes, however, people use words that describe a state of being. For example, someone lying on a desk may be described as "lazy." But lazy isn't a performance. It's a word describing an alleged state of being. Words like nice, genial, and studious, as well as expressions such as "they have a poor attitude" and "he's not motivated" refer to people, rather than describe something that they are doing.

For instance, all of the items in this list qualify as performances:

- Add these numbers
- Ride this bike
- Solve this problem
- Edit this speech
- Play this song
- Divide these numbers
- Draw a duck

These would not qualify as performances:

- Internalize a growing awareness
- Be happy
- Think clearly

- Demonstrate an understanding
- Be safety-conscious
- Have empathy for browbeaten husbands
- Understand physics
- Be concerned with the bottom line
- Be empowered

Here's a little practice. Circle the performance, if any, mentioned in these statements:

1. Without a musical score, sing any of the songs on the following list (list would be added here).

2. Be able to know the principles of behavior modification.

3. Be able to demonstrate an understanding of the principles of aerodynamics.

4. Be able to record blood pressure for an adult patient of any size or weight.

5. Be able to describe verbally the procedure for completing a ballot used in a national election.

Check your responses on the next page.

1. Without a musical score, (sing) any of the songs on the following list (list would be added here).

2. Be able to know the principles of behavior modification.

3. Be able to demonstrate an understanding of the principles of aerodynamics.

4. Be able to (record blood pressure) for an adult patient of any size or weight.

5. Be able to (describe verbally) the procedure for completing a ballot used in a national election.

The performance mentioned in the first item is *sing,* but no performances are stated in Items 2 and 3. Items 4 and 5 state performances; you can tell whether someone is recording blood pressure or describing verbally.

Indicators and Main Intents

Until you know what an objective is really about—its reason for being—you can't select items that will help you find out whether it's been achieved. While the performance stated in the objective is often its main intent, this isn't always the case. Sometimes the objective will state a performance, but it won't be the main intent. Instead, it will describe a way to find out whether the main intent has been accomplished. These performances are called indicator behaviors, because they are intended to indicate whether the main intent was achieved. Here are the definitions of main intents and indicator behaviors:

Main intent (primary intent, principal purpose) is the performance that is the purpose of the objective, i.e., what you want people to be able to do in the real world after they've left the instruction.

Indicator behavior is a visible or audible activity through which the existence of the main intent will be inferred.

Consider this example:

Given a fully equipped surgery, be able to perform a lobotomy on any breed of cockroach.

First question: What's the performance mentioned in the objective? *Perform a lobotomy.* That's what it *says.*

Next question: What's the point (main intent) of the objective? What is the objective mainly about? Why, it is about being able to perform a lobotomy. There is no reason to suspect otherwise. Lobotomizing is the skill the learner is expected to develop.

In this example, the performance stated in the objective is the main intent of the objective. Knowing that, we also know that the only way we can find out if someone has accomplished the objective is to ask that person to perform a lobotomy.

Now let's ask the same two questions of this statement:

Given a series of pictures depicting animals and non-animals, be able to color all the animals.

First question: What's the performance stated in the objective? *Coloring.* That's what it *says.*

Next question: What's the main intent? Why, the objective wants performers to be able to tell the difference between animals and non-animals. It doesn't say so, but in this case it is clear this is the main intent. So the answer to "What is the main intent?" here is "Discriminate *(recognize, differentiate)* between animals and non-animals." How did we know that coloring is an indicator behavior and not a main intent? We asked ourselves whether coloring is what the objective writer wants students to be able to do in the real world after leaving the instruction. It's unlikely that the point of the objective is for students to be able to trundle through life coloring animals.

Why does the objective say *color* when it wants learners to be able to discriminate? Simply because in this case the objective writer decided to state an indicator rather than a main intent. So the stated performance is an indicator, and the main intent is implied.

There is nothing wrong with having an objective state an indicator behavior and not the main intent, *so long as the main intent is clear.*

In this example, you are told to infer from the performers' coloring behavior whether they can tell the difference between animals and non-animals. Because the main intent is clear, you know you are not going to teach the student to color simply because coloring is the performance stated in the objective. You also know that you will not evaluate or grade the student on his or her coloring ability (i.e., you would never say a thing such as "Yes, yes, you can tell the difference between animals and non-animals, all right, but you did a sloppy job of coloring so I'll have to take 10 points off."). The objective isn't about coloring; it is about discriminating. Since the main intent is clear, I wouldn't bother to rewrite the objective; I'd leave it as is and simply make sure I didn't accidentally evaluate the quality of the coloring when evaluating achievement of the main intent.

One more example:

Given a collection of business letters, be able to make a check mark on those conforming to company policy as outlined in the Perfect Policy Manual of 2093.

What performance is actually stated? Make a check mark. That's what it *says*. But is *checkmarking* the point (main intent) of the objective? Does the objective writer expect people to wander through life making check marks? Not likely. So what is the objective really about? What is the main intent? Discriminating, that's what. It's about being able to tell the difference between letters that do, and don't, meet the standards stated in the manual. Though the objective doesn't actually say that, you can be pretty sure that's what it is by reading the indicator behavior.

So again a performance is stated, but it isn't the main intent of the objective. The main intent is discriminating, and the visible behavior selected as the means by which to indicate presence of the intended skill is checkmarking. Whenever you're not sure about whether the performance is an indicator or main intent, ask the objective writer. If that's you, fix the objective.

To check your skill at identifying main intents and indicators, try the items on page 27.

Here's What To Do:

Circle the performance stated, and then check (✓) the appropriate column to the right. Is the *stated* performance an indicator or a main intent?

	MAIN INTENT	INDICATOR
1. Be able to identify the verb in any sentence.	___	___
2. Be able to circle a verb in any sentence.	___	___
3. Given any number of one-dollar bills, be able to mark those that are counterfeit.	___	___
4. Given a group of essays and a set of standards, be able to evaluate the essays according to the standards.	___	___

Check your responses on the following page.

	MAIN INTENT	INDICATOR
1. Be able to (identify the verb) in any sentence.	✓	
2. Be able to (circle a verb) in any sentence.		✓
3. Given any number of one-dollar bills, be able to (mark) those that are counterfeit.		✓
4. Given a group of essays and a set of standards, be able to (evaluate the essays) according to the standards.	✓	

1. This statement asks learners to be able to *identify* verbs. That is the main intent. There is no indicator, and so you don't know how you will know that the identifying was accomplished. Even so, it seems pretty clear that identifying is the main intent.

2. The stated performance is *circling*. But is that the main intent of the objective? No, circling is an indicator by which you will find out if the main intent, probably recognizing, has been accomplished. (It's doubtful that many people earn their living at verb-circling.)

3. This item says *mark*, but it is clear that the main intent is for someone to be able to recognize a counterfeit one-dollar bill.

4. The performance stated is *evaluate*. That's what it says. It doesn't state, or even hint, at what visible behavior might be acceptable as evidence of evaluating, but it seems clear that evaluating is the main intent. If you think evaluating is an abstraction rather than a performance, follow the rule; i.e., either fix the objective yourself or get its writer to do so.

Overt and Covert

The third and final distinction you need to be able to make is between performances that are visible (overt) and performances that are invisible (covert). Why is this distinction important? Because that's how you will know when to look for indicator behaviors in the objective.

For example, suppose an objective says that someone needs to be able to identify, and that identifying is the main intent. So far, so good. But identifying is a covert (invisible) activity. You could stand perfectly still at an airport while identifying all the brown bags that walk by, and no one would ever know you were doing it. For someone to find out that you're identifying, you'd have to do something visible, such as pointing. Pointing is an indicator behavior through which someone could infer that you did your invisible identifying correctly or incorrectly.

The rule here is simple: When the objective states a covert performance, make sure it also states an indicator. If it doesn't, then someone will have to repair the objective before you can match test items to it.

For a bit of practice in distinguishing between overt and covert performances, look at the next page.

Below are a few words describing various actions. Some are directly visible and some are not. Check (✓) those that are directly visible or audible, those about which you can say, "When people are doing that, I can see or hear them doing it."

1. State   _____

2. Acquire   _____

3. Write   _____

4. Draw   _____

5. Recognize   _____

6. Solve   _____

7. Recall   _____

Check your responses on the following page.

1. **State.** Overt. You can tell if someone is stating something.

2. **Acquire.** Covert or overt, depending on what is being acquired. Acquiring a concept is covert; acquiring a wallet is overt. (Words can be sneaky, can't they?)

3. **Write.** Overt. You can tell directly when someone is writing.

4. **Draw.** Overt or covert. Drawing a picture is overt; drawing a conclusion is covert. (Don't blame me for the fact that words don't always have a single meaning or implication.)

5. **Recognize.** Covert. For you to be able to tell whether someone *recognized,* he or she would have to do something other than recognize—such as point a finger, say something, or write a note.

6. **Solve.** Covert. Similar to adding. Both can be done invisibly.

7. **Recall.** Covert. I can recall all sorts of things and easily hide the fact that I am doing it. If you want to know if someone has recalled something, you need an indicator—an overt behavior that will signal the recalling.

Continue to the next page.

Now it's time to attack the objective/item matching procedure directly.

How To Do It

NOTE: When decoding an objective, the quickest and surest way is to use a pencil to draw a circle around the "doing" word and then to underline any conditions that may be stated.

STEP ONE. Circle the performance stated in the objective.

This means no more than noting the word or phrase that tells what students will be doing when demonstrating their achievement of the objective. Most of the time this is easy to do. When it is more difficult, it is because of a gray area between performances and abstractions or because the "objective" doesn't state any performance at all.

Let's look at a few simple examples, just to be sure we are thinking about the same thing.

Here's What To Do:

Draw a circle around the explicit *performance* (the doing word), if any, mentioned in the following statements:

1. Be able to write the symbols for any twenty electronic components.

2. Be able to demonstrate an understanding of modern poetry.

3. Be able to multiply pairs of two-digit numbers.

4. Be able to show a knowledge of the basic elements of a contract.

Turn the page to check your responses.

1. *Be able to write the symbols for any twenty electronic components.*

   The performance stated is write the symbols. That's what it says. Never mind for the moment whether writing is what the objective is really about. For the moment we are only concerned with whether any kind of performance is stated at all.

2. *Be able to demonstrate an understanding of modern poetry.*

   No performance is stated. The word demonstrate doesn't qualify. What would someone be doing when demonstrating an understanding? Running? Jumping? Writing? Explaining? We can't tell. The word demonstrate sounds like a performance, but that's all.

3. *Be able to multiply pairs of two-digit numbers.*

   This item asks students to multiply. Multiplying qualifies as a performance (as would similar intellectual skills), because we can determine directly whether the multiplying occurred.

4. *Be able to show a knowledge of the basic elements of a contract.*

   No performance is stated. What would someone be doing when "Showing a knowledge of . . ."? Delivering a speech? Writing an essay? Describing contracts? It doesn't say.

To recap, the first step in selecting test items appropriate for measuring accomplishment of an objective is to note the performance mentioned in the objective. When no performance is stated, the statement isn't an objective, and you must either get clarification from whomever wrote the statement, clarify it yourself, or throw it away. Without a performance, there is little sense going on to the next step.

Step One.   Circle the performance stated in the objective.

STEP TWO. If the performance is an indicator, identify the main intent.

If the main intent is clear, then that's all there is to this step. If not, you will need to ask the objective writer for clarification. For example, in the following statement it is clear that the performance called for is an indicator. But what is the main intent?

Given any page of non-technical prose, be able to circle dangling participles.

Why should one be able to circle these things? Surely a person won't be expected to go through life circling danglers. Circling is just an indicator that shows a learner can do something meaningful. But what? Perhaps he or she is expected to be able to recognize or identify dangling participles. That would be my guess. But I could be wrong. It may be that the objective writer wants students to be able to write grammatically correct sentences and is using circling (incorrectly) as a means of finding out whether they can do so. The point is simply that we are not sure. When you can't easily tell what the objective is all about, ask or fix. The example on dangling participles might be rewritten as follows:

Given any page of non-technical prose, be able to identify (circle) dangling participles.

Step One.   Circle the performance stated in the objective.

Step Two.   If the performance is an indicator, identify the main intent.

STEP THREE. If the stated performance is the main intent, note whether it is overt or covert.

If the main intent is a visible or audible performance, you're finished decoding for now. If, on the other hand, the main intent is covert, you'll have to make sure an indicator is stated and that the indicator is the simplest available.

Figure 1 on the opposite page offers a visible picture of the situation. It shows that a performance can be:

1. An **overt main intent** (visible or audible).

    (Examples: writing, marking, singing, kicking, and screaming.)

2. A **covert main intent** (invisible).

    (Examples: identifying, recalling, solving, adding.)

3. An **overt indicator** (visible or audible).

    (Indicators are always overt.)

	OVERT	COVERT
MAIN INTENT	1 Match main intent	2 ADD and match indicator
INDICATOR	3 Match indicator	4 ✕

Figure 1

In Figure 1, the box representing "covert indicator" is crossed out because that category is an absurdity. An indicator can't indicate anything if it's invisible. Here's what to do for each of the three situations:

Visible (overt) main intent. When the performance stated in an objective is a main intent and is observable (visible or audible), then you've finished decoding the objective. Test items will be selected that ask students to accomplish the stated main intent.

Invisible (covert) main intent. When, instead, the main intent is *not* visible—that is, when the main intent is covert (cognitive, internal, or mental)—add a suitable indicator. Always. The indicator must be added because you can't match test items to something that is invisible. The easiest way to do that is simply to add an indicator behavior in parentheses after the performance, like this:

> *Given a list of statements describing goals and perfor-mances, be able to identify (circle) the performances.*

Indicator behavior. When the performance stated is an indicator, make sure it is appropriate for testing the main intent, because it's possible to select indicators that are wrong for the task they are expected to perform. How do you tell whether an indicator is a good one? By testing the indicator. That's the next step.

Step One.   Circle the performance stated in the objective.

Step Two.   If the performance is an indicator, identify the main intent.

Step Three.   If the stated performance is the main intent, note whether it is overt or covert.

STEP FOUR. For objectives containing an indicator, test the indicator.

To *test the indicator* simply means to answer this question:

Is this indicator the simplest and most direct available and well within the repertoire of the student?

If the answer is "Yes," then the indicator behavior is probably acceptable, and you've finished decoding the objective. If the answer is "No," the indicator needs to be simplified.

Let me illustrate the point with this example, borrowed from an English teacher. The objective was stated like this:

Demonstrate an understanding of the difference between a limerick and a sonnet by writing one of each.

Now watch closely (there's nothing up my sleeve, and at no time do my fingers leave my hands).

First question: What's the performance stated in the objective? *Writing.* That's the doing word.

Second question: What is the main intent of the objective? It's about being able to *recognize the difference* between limericks and sonnets. That's what it says. It's about discrimination. (It doesn't say *what kind* of difference the student should be able to discriminate, but it clearly implies that "being able to tell the difference" is the main intent.)

Third question: If the main intent is to find out whether students can tell the difference between limericks and sonnets, how does the instructor intend to find out if they can do it? Why, the instructor will ask them to *write* one of each. It is clear that writing a limerick and a sonnet is the indicator by which the objective writer intends to tell if the main intent is achieved.

Asking students to *write* sonnets and limericks to find out whether they can tell them apart seems a bit much, don't you think? Many students may be unable to write poems, yet be able to tell the two apart. Surely you can think of an easier, more direct indicator than writing. What will tell us whether students can recognize limericks and sonnets when they see them and that will not require students to do more than tell us which poem fits each category? There are several alternatives.

We could give students a pile of pages, each of which has a limerick or sonnet on it, and ask students to *sort* the pages into two piles—one pile for limericks and one for sonnets. *Anyone* ought to be able to sort pages. Or, we could ask them to poke a pencil through the limericks. Or, we could ask them to make a check mark on the sonnets. Or ask for any number of simple, direct actions (behaviors) that *anyone could be expected to perform.* Each of these indicators would tell us whether the desired discrimination is taking place; each of them would directly assess the main intent, without making it easy to assess something *other* than the main intent.

"Well," you might hear an instructor say to a student, "Sure, you can tell the difference between limericks and sonnets, but you write a lousy sonnet and so I'm going to have to take 20 points off." Or, "OK, you can tell one from another, but you don't *really understand* the difference until you can write one." Balderdash! When the indicator isn't the simplest, most direct one available, and if it isn't well within the present capability of the student, the evaluation of the main intent of the objective will almost invariably be confounded with an evaluation of the student's ability to perform the indicator. How often have you heard things like this:

"Well, you got the problems right, but your handwriting is terrible."

"Your essay said all I wanted it to, but I'll have to mark you down for grammar."

Each such sentiment suggests that academic sneakery has been perpetrated. And that's why it is important to test an indicator—to make sure your test items will test the main intent rather than the indicator.

NOTE: Any indicator will do if it is simple, direct, and well within the ability of the student. In the example of the limericks and sonnets, checkmarking sonnets would be as direct as circling limericks. Each of these indicators is a simpler behavior from which we can directly infer whether the covert main intent has been achieved.

Let's nail down Step Four with a few practice items. On the next right-hand page are some objectives with covert main intents and some form of indicator. To ease your reading burden, I've left off detailed conditions and criteria.

Here's What To Do:

1. For each objective, circle the indicator behavior.

2. If it's the simplest possible, check YES.

3. If not, then check NO and write a better one.

OBJECTIVE	Is the indicator simple and direct?		
	YES	NO	WRITE A BETTER INDICATOR
1. Demonstrate an ability to recognize a user-friendly web page by creating one.	____	____	_____
2. Be able to identify sentences that are statements of bias, assumption, generalization, or conclusion by writing sentences illustrating those categories.	____	____	_____
3. Be able to compute the solution to binary addition problems.			

3. Be able to compute the solution to binary addition problems.

Sample test item:
Describe the steps for solving each of the following binary addition problems:

11000   0101
+11000   +0011

     ____   ____   _____

Turn the page to check your responses.

OBJECTIVE	Is the indicator simple and direct?		
	YES	NO	WRITE A BETTER INDICATOR
1. Demonstrate an ability to recognize a user-friendly web page by creating one.		✓	Point to
2. Be able to identify sentences that are statements of bias, assumption, generalization, or conclusion, by writing sentences illustrating those categories.		✓	Circle the category
3. Be able to compute the solution to binary addition problems. *Sample test item:* Describe the steps for solving each of the following binary addition problems: 11000 0101 +11000 0011		✓	Write the solution

See explanation on the following pages.

Here's the explanation.

1. *Main intent:*   Recognize.

   Indicator: Create.

   Simplest, most direct indicator? No.

The indicator is more complex than required, requiring more skill than called for by the main intent. A better indicator would be to have students point to suitable web pages or to write their initials on them.

2. *Main intent:*   Discriminating statements of bias, etc.

   Indicator: Writing sentences.

   Simplest, most direct indicator? No.

In this example, the indicator would tell you whether the objective has been achieved. But the indicator is by no means the simplest possible; it asks students to do more than needed to indicate their ability to recognize the types of sentences listed. It asks students to *write* a sentence when the objective only wants to know if they can *recognize* a sentence. Several indicators would be less bulky and less demanding of student time. For example, four columns could be drawn to the right of the sentences to be judged, each headed with one of the four judgment categories (i.e., bias, assumption, generalization, conclusion). Students could be asked to read each sentence presented and to check the appropriate column or columns.

3. *Main intent:*   Solving problems.
   Indicator: Describing solution steps.
   Simplest, most direct indicator? No.

(continued on page 46)

Here the main intent and the indicator clearly do not match. It is not possible to determine whether students can solve problems by asking them to describe the steps they would follow in solving the problems. Oh, sure, if they can't describe the steps, you might conclude with some confidence that they can't solve the problems. But if they *can* describe the steps, you cannot conclude that they *can* solve the problems. Describing isn't the same as solving.

What would be a more appropriate indicator? Ask performers to tell or write the solution. Either indicator would be appropriate—more direct and simpler. If you were interested in *how* they arrived at their solution, some other indicator would be called for. The objective, however, relates to outcomes rather than processes.

Caution

Be watchful when the word *identify* is used in an objective; it's a slippery one. You may not be aware that other people are using a different meaning for the same word. For example, *identify* is sometimes used to mean "point to," as in "Identify the bones of the body." This could mean to point to bones on a diagram or to point to the real thing.

Sometimes *identify* means to select a verbal description of the real thing, as in "Identify the correct answers in each of these multiple-choice questions." The word is also used to mean describe or tell, as in "On the paper provided, briefly identify the causes of bankruptcy." Finally, it is sometimes used to mean list, as in "Identify the steps in cashing a check." With all these possible meanings floating around, *identify* should be accompanied by a simple indicator when used as a main intent.

Where We Are

At this point, you should be able to carry out the steps associated with decoding an objective. You should be able to:

1. Identify (circle) the performance stated.

2. When the stated performance is an indicator, identify the main intent.

3. When the main intent is covert, add a suitable indicator behavior.

4. Test the indicator to ensure that it is the simplest and most direct one possible and well within the repertoire of the students.

Now that you can decode objectives, you're ready to begin drafting or selecting test items that will tell you whether your objective has been achieved as you intended.

So let's get to it.

4
Matching the Performances

"So the way you find out how many cows are in the pasture is to count the number of legs and divide by four."

"Why not just count heads directly?"

"Because if you're off just a few legs, you won't be off that many cows."

Dumb, isn't it? And about as useless as my trying to find out how well you write by asking you to answer some multiple-choice questions about writing. About as useless as trying to find out if students can interview by asking them to point to errors in other peoples' interviews. Unless the measuring instrument matches the thing to be measured, we haven't got a chance of learning what we want to know, i.e., whether a student can do whatever an objective requires. To do that, we make sure that each and every item asks for the same performance as the objective, under the conditions described in the objective. This chapter is about matching performances.

Most of the time performance matching takes only a second or so, provided the objective is well stated. It takes a little longer only when the objective is poorly stated. Here's the procedure:

When the performance stated in the objective is:

1. **Main intent and overt**

   Only one type of test item will do. *Ask the student to do that which is called for by the indicator.*

2. **Main intent and covert**

   Add an indicator to the objective: Test to make sure it is simple, direct, and well within the repertoire of the student. *Write or select test items that call for the same or equally simple and direct indicator behavior.*

3. **Indicator and overt**

   Check the main intent. If unclear, fix or discard the objective. If clear, make sure that the indicator is appropriate—simple, direct, and well within student capability. *Write or select test items that call for the same or equally simple and direct indicator behavior.*

4. **Indicator and covert**

   There's no such thing. *Say something tart to the objective writer. Get the objective fixed or discarded.*

Let's explore each of the first three possibilities.

1. **The performance stated in the objective is the main intent and overt.**

	OVERT	COVERT
MAIN INTENT	1 Match main intent	2 ADD and match indicator
INDICATOR	3 Match indicator	4

When the performance stated in the objective is the *main intent* of that objective, and *visible*, prepare or select test items that *ask* students to *perform the main intent of the objective.* No indicator is needed; when the main intent is visible, it is its own indicator. Whatever the main intent, the item must ask students to do it. No other form of the item is acceptable. For example, if the objective says:

> *Be able to ride a unicycle 100 yards on a level, paved surface without falling off,*

the performance stated is *ride a unicycle.* The performance of riding is visible (overt) and is the main intent of the objective. Therefore, the only way to find out if learners have achieved the objective is to ask them to ride. No other form of test item is appropriate, regardless of the "difficulty level." Questions that ask about the history of spokes, a request for an essay on seat appreciation, or multiple-choice questions on nomenclature won't do. The only way you can find out if they can ride is to watch them ride.

Of course, you may want them to ride successfully three times out of four before you will say the objective is achieved (provided that's the criterion stated in the objective), in which case you would have four items or behavior samples. But each and every one of them MUST ask students to ride. If it asks them to do anything else, you will *not know* whether the objective is achieved. Consider this example:

> *Be able to pick open at least four five-pin tumbler locks within twenty minutes.*

What's the performance stated? Picking locks. Is the performance visible? Yes, you can see people picking locks. What is the main intent? Why, lock picking. The objective wants students to be able to open locks of a certain kind by picking them. Would any of the following items be appropriate for assessing the objective?

1. Draw a diagram of a typical pin tumbler.

2. For a five-pin tumbler lock, name the picks you would use in picking it open.

3. Name three people important to the history of the pin tumbler.

4. For each of the locks named on the list below, write the name of the picks most appropriate for speedy opening.

5. Write a short essay on the history of keyholes.

No, not one of those items is appropriate if you want to find out whether students can actually pick. Items such as these may be useful as *diagnostic* items designed to tell you why an objective was not accomplished, but they are useless for telling you whether the objective has been accomplished. To include items like these just because they may make the test more interesting is not playing fair with students. It is simply no good to have items that ask them to pick a little, talk a little. It's got to be pick, pick, pick, or you will never know if the objective has been achieved. And if you don't know whether it has been achieved, you won't be able to show that your instruction is as successful as you believe it is.

NOTE: When the performance mentioned in the objective is OVERT and at the same time the MAIN INTENT, the test item looks almost identical to the objective; the objective describes what students should be able to do, and the test item says, "Do it." But this is true *only* when the main intent is overt. Unfortunately, it is this category of objective that causes some people to mistakenly conclude that there is no difference between objectives and test items. Now you know what to say to such people. Tactfully, of course.

2. **The performance stated in the objective is the main intent, and covert (internal, invisible, mental).**

	OVERT	COVERT
MAIN INTENT	1 Match main intent	2 ADD and match indicator
INDICATOR	3 Match indicator	4 ✕

(continued on page 54)

When the main intent stated in the objective is covert, do this:

1. If the main intent of the objective isn't clear, fix it or junk it.

2. Add an indicator behavior by which accomplishment of the objective can be assessed.

3. Make sure the indicator is the simplest and most direct indicator possible.

4. Note the performance called for by the test item.

5. If that performance is the same, or same type, as the indicator stated in the objective, the performances match and the item is potentially useful. If not, modify or discard the test item.

Let's look at an example. Originally, the objective read like this:

Objective: *Be able to identify verbs in a series of sentences.*

The main intent is "identify," but since there are so many possible meanings, an indicator was added, like this:

Objective: *Be able to identify (underline) the verb in a sentence.*

A test item was drafted to read like this:

Test item: *There are ten sentences on this page. Circle the verb in each.*

First question: What's the *visible* performance stated? *Underlining.*

Second question: Is that the simplest, most direct indicator? Yes. It's one of several that might be used, but it is simple, direct, and well within the student's ability.

Third question: What's the performance called for in the test item? *Circling.*

Last question: Is that the same, or the same *type* of, performance as underlining? Yes. Underlining and circling are two simple ways to *point to* the verbs. Each requires the same amount of skill (or lack of it.)

In this example, therefore, the performance called for by the test item is the "same" as that of the objective, and the item is a good candidate for assessing achievement of the objective. All that remains is to make sure the conditions match, which we'll do in the next chapter. Here's another example:

Objective: *From an array of watchmaking tools, be able to identify those used for winding mainsprings.*

Test item: *Each of the tools laid out on Table 2 has been tagged with a number. On your answer sheet, write the tag number of each of the tools used for winding mainsprings.*

First question: What's the *visible* performance stated in the objective? *There isn't any.* Identifying is a covert performance. So before proceeding, we must add an indicator. After a second or two of thought, we revise the objective as follows:

Objective: *From an array of watchmaking tools, be able to identify* (point to) *those used for winding mainsprings.*

Notice how easy it is to improve the objective by adding a word or two in parentheses, rather than by rewriting the entire statement? Now we have a visible performance and can go on to the next question.

Second question: Is this a simple, direct indicator? Yes. Everybody has *something* they can point with.

Third question: What's the performance called for in the test item? *Writing* a number.

Last question: Is that the same, or same type of, performance as pointing? Close, but no cigar. *If* the target audience (students) can write numbers easily and legibly, then writing numbers would be OK as an indicator behavior. Can you think of an even simpler indicator to use? One that wouldn't require a writing skill? How about the following as possibilities:

- Put the tools used for mainspring winding in the green tray, or

- Remove the tags from the correct tools and hand them to the instructor, or

- Point to the tools used for mainspring winding.

3. **The performance stated in the objective is an indicator.**

	OVERT	COVERT
MAIN INTENT	1 Match main intent	2 ADD and match indicator
INDICATOR	3 Match indicator	4 ✕

When the stated performance is an indicator (and necessarily overt), you'll need to be sure of the main intent before you can successfully decide whether a given test item will be useful. For example:

Objective: *Given completed employment application forms, be able to checkmark those that meet the standards listed in the Guide to Quality Employees.*

Test Item: *List characteristics an applicant must have to meet the standards described in the Guide to Quality Employees.*

What's the point (main intent) of the objective? What does the objective writer actually want people to be able to do once the instruction is over? Probably identify. So let's modify the objective:

Objective: *Given completed employment application forms, be able to identify (checkmark) those that meet the standards listed in the Guide to Quality Employees.*

Now we can try to match the item to the objective.

First question: What's the *visible* performance stated in the objective? *Checkmarking.* That's what it says.

Second question: Is that a simple, direct way to indicate identifying? Yes.

Third question: What's the performance called for in the test item? *List characteristics.*

Last question: Is listing the same as check-marking? Not even close. The item is therefore unacceptable in its present form.

"But," you will hear people say, "If students don't know what characteristics are relevant, they won't be able to select the forms that meet the standards." Probably true. But that's irrelevant, isn't it? The point is that if you want to find out whether students have accomplished the objective, you have to ask them to perform as the objective describes, not to demonstrate what they would need to know *before* performing as desired. In this example, then, the performances called for in the test item and the objective do not match. One or the other needs to be fixed, or the item discarded.

You should now be ready for some practice in matching performances, and so some guided practice is coming up. To help you with your matching, I'll offer three kinds of aids. Take your pick.

A brief summary of what to do in
response to each kind of stated
performance.   *Page 60*

A checklist to remind you of the
steps to follow in matching
item to objective.   *Page 61*

A flowchart that shows the
relationship between the steps
of the matching procedure.
(WARNING: If you are not used to
using flowcharts as a thinking
tool, don't even look at it.)   *Page 62*

The guided practice begins on   *Page 64*

What-To-Do Summary

	OVERT	COVERT
MAIN INTENT	1 *Match main intent*	2 *ADD and match indicator*
INDICATOR	3 *Match indicator*	4 ✕

When the performance stated in the objective is:

1. **Main intent and overt** . . . Ask the student to perform the main intent.
2. **Main intent and covert** . . . Add an indicator to the objective, and test to make sure it is simple, direct, and well within the repertoire of the student. Write or select test items that call for the same or equally simple and direct indicator behavior.
3. **Indicator and overt** . . . If the main intent is unclear, fix or discard the objective. If clear, make sure that the indicator is appropriate — simple, direct, and well within student capability. Write or select test items that call for the same or a similar indicator behavior.
4. **Indicator and covert** . . . No such thing. Sneer at the objective writer (tactfully, of course). Get the objective fixed or junked. (How would you like to have to evaluate someone's accomplishment of this "objective," for example? "Be able to demonstrate an ability to think by recalling the parts of a syllogism." Lotsa luck.)

Objective/Item Matching Checklist*

1. What is the performance stated in the objective?
   • If there isn't any, repair or discard the objective.

2. Is the performance a main intent or an indicator?
   • If you can't tell, revise or discard the objective.

3. If it is an indicator, can you identify the main intent?
   NO . . . revise or discard the objective.
   YES . . . test the indicator against the main intent.

4. If the performance is a main intent, is it overt or covert?
   COVERT . . . add an indicator and test it for simplicity.
   OVERT . . . go to 5.

5. If the performance is overt, does the item performance match?
   YES . . . go to 7.
   NO . . . revise or reject the item or the objective.

6. If the performance in the objective is an indicator, does the performance in the test item match?
   YES . . . go to 7.
   NO . . . revise or reject the item.

7. Do the conditions described in the item match those of the objective?
   NO . . . revise the conditions in the item.
   YES . . . the item is potentially useful for testing accomplishment of the objective.

*A removable copy of this checklist is inserted between the last page and back cover of this book.

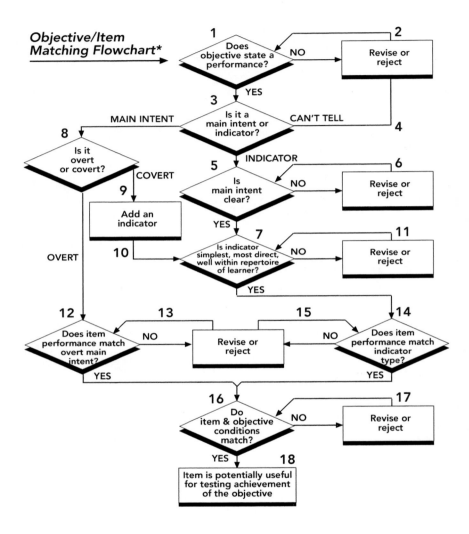

* *A removable copy of this flowchart is inserted between the last page and back cover of this book.*

GUIDED PRACTICE

Here are some practice items that will let you try your hand at matching performances.

Each pair of statements that follows consists of an objective and a test item. Decide YES or NO, according to whether the performance called for by the test item matches that called for by the objective. If you CAN'T TELL whether there is a match because the objective or item doesn't call for a performance, check (✓) the CAN'T TELL column.

> **NOTE:** You will find it easier to decode the objective and item pairs if you *circle the performances* with your pencil as you go. If there is no performance to circle in the objective, it doesn't matter how profound the statement sounds; check CAN'T TELL and go on to the next item.

On the chance that you will be able to move through the practice in a more sprightly manner if I model the procedure, I will invite you to peer into my stream of consciousness as I work through the first practice item.

Turn the page for the practice item and explanation.

Do the performances match?
YES   NO   CAN'T
TELL

---

1. *Objective:* Given a customer's deposit to either a savings or checking account, be able to verify the deposit. (Verify means compare the cash with amount shown on deposit slip, check deposit slip calculations for accuracy, stamp and initial deposit slip after verification.)

    Test Item: Describe how you would respond to this customer comment: "I'd like to make a deposit to my checking account, but I don't know how to fill out these new deposit slips. What do I have to do to deposit $20.00 in cash and a check for $14.79?"

                            ✓

    _____   _____   _____

Thoughts While Matching. "Let's see, now. What's the performance called for by the objective? Well, it says *verify the deposit.* I'll circle that so it won't get away. Is that the main intent or an indicator? Looks like the performance is a main intent. Is it overt or covert? Hmm. I could watch someone verifying deposits directly—counting money, stamping and initialing deposit slips—so I'll say the performance is overt.

"Okay, the performance stated in the objective is an overt main intent. That tells me that there is only one kind of item that will do—one that asks the student to verify deposits. So let's look at the test item. What does it ask the student to do? It says *describe a response to a customer comment.* Oh, oh. Describing a response isn't the same as verifying a deposit. The performances don't match, so I'll put a check in the NO col-umn." (In real life, you would discard or repair the item rather than check a column.)

Now it's your turn.

Do the performances match?
YES   NO   CAN'T
TELL

1. *Objective:* Be able to construct a staircase according to a blueprint and specifications.

   Test Item: Inspect the blueprints and specifications in Envelope A and decide whether they were properly followed in the construction of the staircase labeled Staircase 3.

   _____   _____   _____

2. *Objective:* Support a candidate of your choice in his or her campaign for election to a public office.

   Test Item: Prove that you have supported a candidate of your choice in his or her campaign for election to a public office.

   _____   _____   _____

3. *Objective:* Be able to carry out the booking procedure for an adult violator of any section of the Penal Code that requires taking the subject into custody.

   Test Item: George Spelvin, age 23, male, has been caught in the act of setting fire to an office building (Section 448a, PC). Complete all the steps needed to book the subject.

   _____   _____   _____

Do the performances match?
YES   NO   CAN'T
                  TELL

4. *Objective:* Given   poorly-stated objectives, be able to reword them so that they include a performance, conditions under which the performance will occur, and a criterion of acceptable performance.

   Test Item: The objectives below are in need of work. Reword them so that they meet the criteria of well-stated objectives.   _____   _____   _____

5. *Objective:* Be able to sort accident reports into two piles; those that are complete and those that are incomplete.

   Test Item: Sort the accident reports in Envelope B into "complete" and "incomplete" piles, and circle the missing information on those reports that are incomplete.   _____   _____   _____

Do the performances match?
YES   NO   CAN'T
                        TELL

6. *Objective:* Understand how statistics are used to determine risk and probability.

   Test Item: Describe at least three ways that statistics may be used to determine risk and probability.   _____ _____ _____

7. *Objective:* Given wiring diagrams, be able to identify (name) the item represented by each symbol.

   Test Item: Locate the laminated wiring diagram labeled "Test Diagram D," and write the name of each symbol on the diagram.   _____ _____ _____

Turn the page to check your responses.

Do the performances match?

	YES	NO	CAN'T TELL

1. *Objective:* Be able to construct a staircase according to a blueprint and specifications.

   Test Item: Inspect the blueprints and specifications in Envelope A and decide whether they were properly followed in the construction of the staircase labeled Staircase 3.

   _____   ✓ _____   _____

2. *Objective:* Support a candidate of your choice in his or her campaign for election to a public office.

   Test Item: Prove that you have supported a candidate of your choice in his or her campaign for election to a public office.

   _____   _____   ✓ _____

3. *Objective:* Be able to carry out the booking procedure for an adult violator of any section of the Penal Code that requires taking the subject into custody.

   Test Item: George Spelvin, age 23, male, has been caught in the act of setting fire to an office building (Section 448a, PC). Complete all the steps needed to book the subject.

   ✓ _____   _____   _____

1. No match. Inspecting a staircase is not the same as constructing one. If you want to know if students can construct a staircase, then you must ask each of them to construct one. There is no other way to determine whether they can do it. If it is impractical or impossible to have them do it, have them do the next best thing, perhaps build models of a staircase, and then *infer* whether students have achieved the objective.

   Remember that inferences are risky; they are even more risky if the consequences of not achieving the objective are perilous. (Your students may be able to build models of a staircase but may not be able to build one of actual size that meets safety specifications.)

2. Can't tell. Neither the objective nor the test item describes a performance. What is someone doing when supporting a candidate? Propping the person up? Contributing to the campaign fund? Speaking in the candidate's favor? Unless you know the performances that define *supporting,* you can't decide how to test the objective.

3. A match. The objective wants trainees to be able to carry out the booking procedure, and that's what the item asks them to do. The item is appropriate for finding out if the objective has been achieved. Will one item be enough? Should several similar items be used? This, and similar issues, will be discussed in Chapter 6.

Do the performances match?

	YES	NO	CAN'T TELL

4. *Objective:* Given poorly-stated objectives, be able to reword them so that they include a performance, conditions under which the performance will occur, and a criterion of acceptable performance.

   Test Item: The objectives below are in need of work. Reword them so that they meet the criteria of well-stated objectives.   ✓ ____ ____ ____

5. *Objective:* Be able to sort accident reports into two piles; those that are complete and those that are incomplete.

   Test Item: Sort the accident reports in Envelope B into "complete" and "incomplete" piles, and circle the missing information on those reports that are incomplete.   ____ ✓ ____ ____

6. *Objective:* Understand how statistics are used to determine risk and probability.

   Test Item: Describe at least three ways that statistics may be used to determine risk and probability.   ____ ____ ✓ ____

7. *Objective:* Given wiring diagrams, be able to identify (name) the item represented by each symbol.

   Test Item: Locate the laminated wiring diagram labeled "Test Diagram D," and write the name of each symbol on the diagram.   ✓ ____ ____ ____

4. A match. The objective asks that students be able to re-word objectives, and that's exactly what the test item asks them to do. So the performances match.

5. The objective says sort, but it's clear that the (unstated) main intent is to be able to recognize complete and incomplete reports. The test item also asks for sorting. So far, so good. But the item *also* asks for students to circle missing information. Hmm. How can you circle information if it's missing? So the item asks for more in the way of skill than does the objective (and more than is humanly possible).This is like those situations where you're told, "Oh, sure. You got the right answers, but you didn't show your work." No match.

6. Can't tell. Until a performance is stated in the objective, there's no way of knowing whether "describing" is a suitable way to find out whether the non-stated performance has been achieved. The correct response here is to fix the objective or throw it away.

7. A match. The objective states the main intent (identify) and adds an indicator by which you can tell whether the identifying was done (name). But the test item asks the student to "write the name" on the diagram, and the objective just says "name." So the item asks for more skill (writing) than does the objective, but writing is a skill that the student knows.

Now that you've had practice in matching performances, it's time to move on to the second part of the process, that of matching the conditions. This is where you'll get to smite, smote, and skewer another potential source of instructional sneakiness.

Go get 'em !

5
Matching the Conditions

Suppose you are enrolled in a penmanship course and are working to accomplish the objective of writing capital letters that conform to a specified size standard. You practice diligently on all the scratch paper you can find and begin to feel pretty confident with the grand flow of your letters. Then, when exam time comes around, you are handed the following test item:

> *Write the letters of the alphabet in capital letters. Write them on the slab of butter placed beneath 6 inches of water in the bottom of Sink 3. Write with the wooden stylus provided.*

The ensuing conversation with the instructor might sound something like this:

> "Wait a minnit. The objective said I need to be able to write capital letters."
> "Correct. And that's precisely what the test item asks you to do."
> "But it says I gotta do it on a slab of butter *under water!*"
> "Come now. *Anybody* can write letters on *paper*. You don't

really understand how to do it unless you can do it under water. That's the *real* test."

"But the objective didn't say anything about water."

"It doesn't have to. It's obvious that I should be allowed to ask you to write on any surface I select. Besides, I'm testing for transfer."

Having decided that the job market for underwater writers is probably limited, you now register for a course in TV repair. During this course you are expected to accomplish the following objective:

With all parts, tools, and diagrams available, be able to assemble any antenna found in the 1999 Bleak and Dreary catalog.

After properly shredding your fingertips and dripping solder on your lap, you finally feel ready to show what you have learned. When you announce your readiness to demonstrate your skill, you are given a piece of paper that says:

On the lab table you will find a package labeled "A," containing the parts and diagram needed to assemble a common TV antenna. Using any tools of your choice, assemble the antenna on the roof of the shop garage and mount it on top of the 50-foot tower.

The ensuing discussion might go something like this:

"Now, see here, kind sir, this test item appears not to be consistent with the objective."

"Oh?"

"Yes, indeed. It appears that the objective tells me to be able to assemble an antenna . . ."

"And that's *exactly* what the test item asks you to do."

"Please, sir, but I beg to differ. The item says I must do the assembling on the roof of the garage, which, as we all know, slopes."

"So?"

"Well, sir, I did all my assembly practice on the floor of the shop. Quite different conditions, you know."

"Oh? Do you think you're going to have a nice level shop floor handy every time you want to put an antenna together?"

"Of course not, sir . . ."

"Well, then, what're you complaining about?"

"Simply that I was not apprised of the conditions under which I would be ultimately expected to perform. Unless you tell me what you, as the expert, think I should be able to do, how will I know what to practice?"

"How could you get this far in the course without knowing that you put antennas together on roofs and not on shop floors?"

"Easily, sir."

"Oh, how?"

"I just believed what I read in the objectives you gave me."

Clearly, the conditions called for in the test item were different from those called for in the objective. And readers of this scenario must admire your restraint in not mentioning to the instructor that the test item actually asked for a skill in addition to the one stated in the objective. The objective asked you to assemble, and the item asked you to *assemble* and *mount*.

Though these examples may seem rather bizarre (they were chosen for that purpose), you will probably remember even stranger ones as you think back over your years as a student— if you ever saw an objective at all.

Matching Conditions

So far, you have seen that to find out whether students have achieved an objective, your test items must ask them to do what the objective asks them to do.

The item must also ask students to perform under the same conditions the objective prescribes. If it doesn't, you may learn that students can do *something,* but you will not learn whether they have achieved the objective. If, for example, you want to know if students can make change in the presence of harried customers, you will never find that out if you ask them to make change only in a quiet classroom. You might *predict* that skills learned under quiet conditions will transfer to those of turmoil and anxiety, but you won't know for sure.

Thus, the conditions under which testing is performed should be the same as those called for in the objective.

What's a Condition?

A condition is anything that will impact on the shape of a performance, anything that will make a difference in how the performance is executed. For example, if a student is given a set of tools or instruments to aid the performance, that's a condition that would influence the way the performing is done. People who are making sales presentations with the aid of a sales outline and/or an actual product would make the presentations differently than if these conditions were not present.

Conditions, therefore, are the things that competent performers have available to them while they are performing, as well as environmental features that might influence the nature of the performance. (Students should have the same conditions while learning and demonstrating their competence.) The objective should state all the conditions that might have a significant impact on how the performance is carried out. If there is any sort of "trick" to deciding which conditions to provide while testing, do it by answering this question: "What things and environmental features will I have to provide before the student can practice the objective?"

How To Do It

1. Read the conditions stated in the objective.

2. Arrange for the test item to be administered under the same conditions, or under conditions as close to the objective as you can manage.

For example, consider the following objective:

Given an automobile that has just received scheduled maintenance, be able to road test the car and complete road test report RTR-3A. Criteria: The tested car is not damaged or the interior soiled; the road test report is complete and legible.

You already know how to identify (circle) the performance. In this case there are two: road testing and report completion. So the test item will ask for road testing and report completion. What about the conditions? Well, you'll need to provide the testee with an automobile and a copy of report RTR-3A. So your test item might look like this:

Test item: *Envelope D contains a copy of RTR-3A. Road test the black 1929 Ford Sedan in stall 12, and complete the road test report. Make sure you refrain from soiling the car interior in any way and that your completed report is legible.*

The rule for matching conditions is the same as for matching performances: *Make sure that the test items are administered under the same conditions (no more, no less) as are called for by the objective.*

NOTE: Notice that the criteria stated in the objective are included in the above test item. Should test items *always* state criteria? No. You may want to include them as reminders, but most of the time it would make the item too wordy.

Here are a few practice items. First you'll practice detecting whether conditions in test items and objectives match, after which we'll consider what to do when it's not possible to provide test conditions that exactly match those of the objectives.

Practice Items

Below are pairs of statements, each consisting of an objective and a potential test item. Check (✓) the appropriate column to the right, depending on whether the conditions in the item match conditions in the objective:

Do the conditions match?
YES   NO

1. *Objective:* Be able to introduce yourself to a peer in a suitable manner (i.e., look the person in the face, offer a firm handshake, give your name, repeat his or her name when it is given, express pleasure at making his or her acquaintance).

   Test Item: The instructor will point to various members of the class. Introduce yourself to them in a suitable manner.

2. *Objective:* Given each of the following products (list attached), be able to describe to an uninterested prospective customer the features and benefits of each product.

   Test Item: Here's what to do:

   1. Read the product literature in Envelope A.

   2. Describe the features and benefits of each product to your classroom partner.

3. *Objective:* Given a person with a first-degree burn on any part of his or her body, be able to apply first aid using the steps outlined in the Red Cross manual for treatment of first-degree burns.

   Test Item: Instructor points to patient lying on table with midsection exposed and says, "This patient has a first-degree burn on her posterior. Treat it according to the Red Cross manual."

Turn the page to check your responses.

Do the conditions match?
YES   NO

1. *Objective:* Be able to introduce yourself to a peer in a suitable manner (i.e., look the person in the face, offer a firm handshake, give your name, repeat his or her name when it is given, express pleasure at making his or her acquaintance).

    Test Item: The instructor will point to various members of the class. Introduce yourself to them in a suitable manner. ✓

2. *Objective:* Given each of the following products (list attached), be able to describe to an uninterested prospective customer the features and benefits of each product.

    Test Item: Here's what to do:

    1. Read the product literature in Envelope A.

    2. Describe the features and benefits of each product to your classroom partner. ✓

3. *Objective:* Given a person with a first-degree burn on any part of his or her body, be able to apply first aid using the steps outlined in the Red Cross manual for treatment of first-degree burns.

    Test Item: Instructor points to patient lying on table with midsection exposed and says, "This patient has a first-degree burn on her posterior. Treat it according to the Red Cross manual." ✓

1. A match. The performances match—both test item and objective ask the student to exhibit the same performance. And the condition? Well, the objective just says the student is expected to be able to introduce himself or herself to peers. It doesn't specify any special or unusual conditions under which the introducing is to occur. The test items ask for the performance in a classroom. That is acceptable, inasmuch as there is nothing in the objective to suggest otherwise.

2. No match. First, the objective says you will have each of the products available while describing their features and benefits. The test item provides only literature about the products.

   Second, the objective says you need to be able to do your describing to an uninterested prospective customer. The test item asks you to do your describing to your partner.

   Thus, the item describes what might be a useful practice situation in the classroom, but it does not describe a situation that will tell you whether the objective has been achieved.

3. A match. Both objective and test item ask for application of first aid to a person with a first-degree burn. The question of how many items of this type may be needed to adequately test for competence will be discussed a little later.

Turn the page for three more practice items.

More Practice Items

Do the conditions match?

	YES	NO

4. *Objective:* Given any model of Disaster Master aircraft, be able to remove and replace any engine part.

   Test Item: On Table 3 are engines from three different Disaster Master aircraft and a new engine part for each. For each engine, remove the old part and replace it with the new.

| _____ | _____ |

5. *Objective:* For a blouse made of any material, be able to repair bad stitches or skipped stitches.

   Test Item: Inspect the pile of clothing on Table 4 and repair any incorrect work.

| _____ | _____ |

6. *Objective:* Be able to multiply correctly any pair of two-digit numbers.

   Test Item: Without using a calculator, multiply the following pairs of two-digit numbers (numbers added).

| _____ | _____ |

Do the conditions match?

         YES   NO

---

4. *Objective:* Given any model of Disaster Master aircraft, be able to remove and replace any engine part.

   Test Item: On Table 3 are engines from three different Disaster Master aircraft and a new engine part for each. For each engine, remove the old part and replace it with the new.   ✓

5. *Objective:* For a blouse made of any material, be able to repair bad stitches or skipped stitches.

   Test Item: Inspect the pile of clothing on Table 4 and repair any incorrect work.   ✓

6. *Objective:* Be able to multiply correctly any pair of two-digit numbers.

   Test Item: Without using a calculator, multiply the following pairs of two-digit numbers (numbers added).   ✓

4. No match. The objective says the student needs to be able to do something to an *aircraft;* specifically, to take out and replace engine parts. The item asks the student to take out and replace parts in engines that are *sitting on a table.* If you have ever looked under the hood of a car or tried to work on an engine there, you know that working on an engine mounted in a car is quite different from working on one sitting on a table. So the performances match, but the conditions don't.

5. No match. There are two problems with this pair of statements. First, though both the objective and test item ask the student to be able to repair, the objective expects to see the skill of "repairing bad or skipped stitches," while the test item asks to see the skill of "repairing *any* incorrect work." Thus, though both use the word "repair"—thereby lulling us into thinking the performances match—the test item asks for more skill than the objective.

   Second, the conditions don't match. The objective wants the student to be able to apply his or her skill to blouses; the test item, to unspecified types of clothing. You may think the difference trivial, but only if you've never been faced with test items that ask for something different from what you were led to expect.

6. No match. The objective is concerned with correct multiplication, rather than with the means by which the multiplication is done. The test item provides a restriction (no calculator) not required by the objective.

   Again, this pair exemplifies that all-too-common situation in which a test requires more, or different, skills than called for by the objective. Don't put up with it. It's not a professional practice.

Approximations

Sometimes the *"match the conditions in the items with the conditions in the objective"* rule must be bent, and, occasionally, twisted literally out of shape.

Consider this objective, from a course on how to repair atomic bombs at Hypothetical U (now known as Crater Lake II):

> *When faced with a malfunctioning atomic bomb of 10 kilotons or less, and shown one symptom, be able to repair the malfunction. Repair must be completed within 45 minutes, and the bomb must function within manufacturer's specifications.*

As you must guess, it might be somewhat impractical to create a test in which the student is given a live bomb with a "bug" in it. Making the conditions on the test match the conditions of the objective might be somewhat foolhardy. The consequence of an error is just potentially too great. After all, this doesn't seem to be a situation in which a serious error is likely to be followed by little more than an embarrassed "Oops."

It's clear what the objective wants—it wants students to be able to fix troubles in real bombs. So far, so good. And to find out if students can fix troubles, you must ask them to fix troubles. That's clear, too. But in this case it's too dangerous to let them demonstrate their skill on the real thing (the students might get a little testy). What can you do?

You can simulate. You can approximate. You can give the students some sort of pretend bomb and ask them to do what the objective wants them to do. If they can do it with the pretend bomb, you will have to *assume* they can do it with the real thing. Is that a safe assumption? Depends on how closely your conditions match those of the objective. If you only have to *approximate* one condition, your guess as to whether they will be able to perform under the real conditions will be better than if you have to approximate two or more. If, for example, bomb repair is done under stressful conditions and you watch students repair in the cool, cool, cool of the evening, you should be less confident of their ability to do it "out there" than if you had provided some real stress during the performance on the pretend bomb.

Two points. First, *never* simulate *performance*. Always ask your students to do that which the objective asks them to do, even though you must provide simulated conditions. Second, remember that when you simulate or approximate conditions, you will have to make *inferences* about whether students will be able to do the "real thing" asked for by the objective. You will have to make an educated guess about whether the objective has been achieved, after watching performance under other-than-appropriate conditions.

Sometimes we can provide conditions close to those called for by the objective, and sometimes the conditions will be considerably different from those called for by the objective. Suppose, for another example, that the objective says something like this:

Be able to rescue a drowning person.

If you want to find out whether the objective has been achieved, it's pretty clear that you will have to simulate the conditions. I suppose you and your students could hang around the beaches waiting for the right moment, but that would be inefficient—not to mention dangerous if your students aren't very competent yet. So some approximation would have to do. What kind of approximation? The closest approximation to the real thing that you can arrange. Multiple-choice questions on the history of drowning won't work, nor will having them describe how they would save an unfortunate drowning person. You can do better than that. You could provide them with someone pretending to need help and ask each student to perform the desired task. That is, wherever possible, ask students to perform the *main intent,* even though the conditions under which the performance is exhibited are somewhat different from those that represent the real thing.

Consider poor Dr. Harry Lymph, professor of medicine, who wants to know if his students can perform an appendectomy. He can't just run down to the street and accost strangers with, "Hi, there. Mind having your appendix out?" If he doesn't have enough patients to go around, he must do some approximating.

As one alternative, he could find out if students can perform each of the sub-skills separately. For example, he could ask each student to show on a real person where the incision would be made, show and describe how to use retractors, how to tie the knots, and so on. But while that would tell him whether subordinate objectives were achieved, it wouldn't tell him if students could actually perform an appendectomy. It would not qualify as a simulation or an approximation of an appendectomy, because the skills called for in any of the items testing a piece of the performance is not the same as that called for in the objective. *Unless performances match, you can't conclude you are approximating.*

So what can the poor professor do? Well, he could use one of the mannequins that have been created for use in surgery simulations, asking each student to remove the appendix of the mannequin. Learners would be demonstrating the desired skills, but under conditions somewhat different from those faced with a live patient.

He might also ask each student to remove the appendix from a cadaver. Here again, learners would be performing the relevant skills, but under conditions different from those faced with live patients. Then, after observing the performance of students in the simulation situation, he would *infer* what each student will be able to do with real patients. Since he hasn't observed students performing the objective, he wouldn't *know* for sure they can perform as desired, but the basis of his inferences would be much more sound than if they were based on the answers to multiple-choice or true-false test items.

When it is a small approximation—that is, when conditions are very close to those called for in the objective—it is a small inference, a small leap. For instance, if the objective says:

> *Be able to select (collect) from the storeroom those instruments and equipment needed to perform an appendectomy,*

and if the test item says:

> *From the array of instruments located on Table 5, collect the instruments used in the performance of an appendectomy and put them into the green tray marked "A",*

the performances match, but the conditions don't. Selecting tools from a table is not the same as selecting them from a storeroom. The difference is so small, however, that you aren't taking much of a risk in using this type of item. That is, if students can select tools from a table, it is a pretty small risk to assume they can select them from a storeroom. The inference is a small one.

But suppose the test item said:

> *On the following page are sketches of a variety of surgical instruments. Check those that are used in the performance of an appendectomy.*

Again, the performances match (both objective and item ask learners to select instruments from "givens"), but the conditions don't. The objective says select from a storeroom, and the item says select from sketches. The inferential leap is larger. The hope is that if students can recognize sketches on paper, they can also recognize the real thing in a storeroom. But the leap from sketches on paper to instruments in storeroom is larger than the leap from instruments on table to instruments in storeroom. Why? Because sketches of instruments are not the same as the instruments themselves. Sketches are only representations of that which students are expected to recognize. As the conditions become less and less like those described in the objective, the size of the inferential leap increases.

Perhaps I can clarify this point with Figure 2. Shown on the far left is the performance called for by the objective. If a test item asks for that performance directly, under the conditions described in the objective, there is no simulation or approximation, and one can decide directly whether the objective has been achieved.

The boxes behind the left-hand box show conditions progressively *less* like that called for by the objective.

- Selecting instruments from a table is a little less like selecting them from a storeroom;
- Selecting instruments from a virtual-reality display of a storeroom is a little less like selecting real instruments from a table;
- Selecting sketches of instruments is still less direct than selecting the real thing;
- Selecting verbal descriptions of instruments is considerably different from selecting the real thing;
- Selecting codes or symbols of the real thing (such as a verbal description written in Morse code) is about as far from the intention of the objective as I can imagine.

The farther one moves to the right in Figure 2, the greater the difference between *observed* performance and *intended* performance (as described by the objective). Thus, the farther one moves to the right, the greater the inference from the performance you see to the performance you *want*.

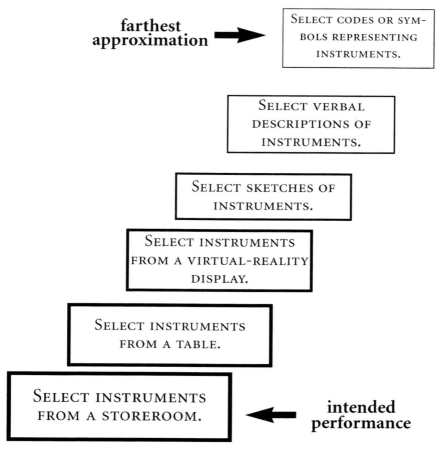

Figure 2.   As approximations increase, the "size" of the inferential leap increases.

Consequence of an Error

How large an inference can you tolerate? *It depends on the consequence of an error.* If the consequence of *not* performing as desired is tolerable, then a larger inference is tolerable. If the consequence of not performing as desired is *serious,* then a large inference (large difference between conditions in item and objective) is risky and should not be tolerated.

In the present example, the consequence of not being able to perform an appendectomy properly can be as large as the loss of a life. While such a loss is not nearly as great as the consequence of a commercial pilot's inability to land a planeload of passengers safely, the loss of life is always a serious consequence. When the potential consequence can be this large, it is important to have students demonstrate their achievement of the objective before certifying them to perform on their own.

If the objective describes an ability to add, on the other hand, and the consequence of an error is only that a little time will be lost or that inappropriate change will be made, you wouldn't have to be excruciatingly diligent in making the test conditions match those of the objective.

So whenever you are unable to make the conditions in the test item match the conditions in the objective, ask yourself:

How serious is the consequence of an error?

The seriousness of the consequence(s) of poor performance will tell you how much energy and budget to invest in matching the test-item conditions to those of the objective.

Dodge City

Some people use some strange dodges or arguments to justify use of items that don't match their objectives. It doesn't seem to matter that by doing so they prevent themselves from finding out whether their objectives are achieved. Here are some common examples:

"But I like my tests to be interesting."

"I like to use a *variety* of items in my tests."

"Well, sure the objective says learners need to be able to DO it, but they don't really understand it unless they can _____ (define it, describe it, tell the history of it, write an essay on it, teach it, etc.)."

"I don't have time to test."

"I don't have the budget needed to arrange real conditions."

"My company has a policy against testing."

My reply to these attempts to weasel is simple and persistent: *If the items don't match the objective, you won't know if the objective has been achieved.* Moreover, if the consequence of an error is serious, you can run some pretty big risks with the lives of your students, as well as those of innocent bystanders. Make your test as interesting as you want, but not at the expense of items that match.

What's Your Pleasure?

You have now practiced all the pieces of the objective/item matching skill. Now you'll be offered some guided practice to put it all together (i.e., you've practiced the steps—now it's time to practice the entire dance).

In addition to the practice, there are two other options I'd like to offer. Though the purpose of the book is to consider only the issue of how to recognize test items relevant to assessing achievement of an objective, there are some related questions buzzing around that I'd like to discuss. Though I may not answer the one(s) distressing you the most, I'd like to try my hand at three or four of them. These are covered in Chapter 6, "Peripheralia."

The other option is to go directly to the skill check (criterion test) in Chapter 8, "Got a Match?" What's your pleasure?

6
Peripheralia

No matter how we try to confine ourselves to a specific topic, there are always loose ends, related issues, and questions. It's rather like trying to explain in detail the workings of some part of the body. Invariably there are questions about how a particular part connects to, interacts with, and influences the functioning of other parts. Though I would like to simply fold up my keyboard at this point and send you off into the exciting practice chapter, I feel a need to deal with a few pieces of peripheralia—oddments that have something to do with testing. They're important issues, but they're not strictly related to the task of matching items to objectives.

How Many Items?

A question that arises when drafting skill checks is "How many items should I use?"

The short answer is, "It depends."

Range of Conditions

The number of times you will need to ask students to perform (i.e., the number of test items you will need) will depend on the range of conditions under which the performance will be expected to occur. If there is only one condition, one or two items should suffice. If, on the other hand, the objective asks for performance under a range of conditions, more items may be needed. The rule is:

Use as many test items as you need to sample the range of conditions.

When should you do that? Whenever the student is expected to (a) use the same things under different conditions when performing or (b) use different things under the same or different conditions when performing. For example, suppose the objective says:

Be able to ride any unicycle 100 yards on a level surface without falling off.

And suppose that "Pedals" Purplin brings her own unicycle to the test situation and rides up a storm. Would you agree that she has achieved the objective? If you said "No," you are right. For one thing, one of the conditions requires her to be able to ride any unicycle, and so far, she's only shown that she can ride one kind. How many kinds would she have to ride before you would be willing to agree that she can ride "any" kind?

The answer is, as many as it takes to sample the range of conditions. There are tall unicycles and squat ones. Some with large wheels and some with small ones. You might say to yourself, "If she can ride a tall one and a short one, I'd be willing to judge that she can ride everything else in between." In this case, you would use two test items to sample the range of conditions. On the other hand, you might say, "Wait a minute. If I have to certify her as being able to ride any unicycle, I would want to see her ride a wider variety than just a tall one and a short one." In that case you would use more items to sample the range of conditions. But each and every such item would ask her to ride a unicycle.

Here's another example. Suppose the objective says:

Given a customer attempting to return merchandise, be able to complete the merchandise return procedure without irritating the customer.

Would one demonstration of the performance suffice to tell you whether someone had achieved the objective? Again, no. Why not? Because customers vary greatly. Some are calm, some are angry. Some speak clearly, some don't. Some have accents, and some have chips on their shoulders. Knowing that, how many customers would students have to deal with to cause you to conclude that they've achieved the objective? Enough to sample the range of conditions. (In this instance, three or four should do.)

Police officers have to learn when to shoot and when not to shoot. But there are many different kinds of situations in which they might find themselves. What would it take to convince you that a given police officer knew when to shoot and when not to shoot? (You can answer that question only if you know the range of possible conditions and which of those conditions are most common.)

Suppose an objective wants students to be able to land a plane on any serviceable airstrip. (Hooray for simulators, wherein faulty performance doesn't kill the student or the customer.) How many test items would you need? Enough for you to sample the range of serviceable airstrips. If students were expected to make those landings in a variety of weather conditions, then different weather conditions would have to be sampled as well. During each test item the student would be doing the same thing, i.e., landing a plane, but the conditions would vary from item to item.

Here is one final example of an objective that contains a range of conditions.

Given a soldering gun, solder, and flux, be able to replace any given component in the Model 10 Brainwasher.

In this case students would be using the same tool no matter which component they were replacing. But there are undoubtedly differences in the conditions under which the replacement must be accomplished. If you have never seen the Model 10 Brainwasher, I can assure you that some components need to be replaced in tight spaces, and some components need to be replaced while the replacer is almost standing on his or her head. So to find out if the objective is achieved, you would need to ask students to replace components in as many parts of the machine as are needed to represent the range of conditions under which the replacement is expected to be done.

It wouldn't be necessary, or practical, to ask for performance under *all* possible combinations of conditions, of course. That's why you are urged to sample the *range* of conditions. Just make sure that each and every item used matches the objective.

What Would Satisfy You?

If, even with an infinite number of perfectly elegant items, you *still* wouldn't be willing to certify as competent each student who performs well on those items, there is something wrong either with your objective or your items. It's no good to say, "Even if students perform well on these ten items, I still wouldn't be willing to say they've achieved the objective." If that's your feeling, your test construction isn't finished. Take another look at the objective, especially at its main intent, because the trouble is likely to be there. The trouble is probably that the objective doesn't accurately describe what it is you *really* want students to be able to do. If there is something *more* you want students to do than is expressed by your items, it is likely that the objective needs revision.

The Rule of Reason

While we're on the subject of "how many items make a test," it would be well to mention the rule of reason relating to item range. It is terribly tempting to create bizarre or improbable items when an objective describes a range of givens or conditions. "Oh, well," the argument often goes, "they don't really understand those problems unless they can solve them while being strung up by their toes," or "they can't really be said to know how to diagnose illness unless they can recognize symptoms of Martian malady and Diddlefinger's disease," or "they really don't know how to troubleshoot unless they can solve problems that may occur only once in a lifetime."

Sometimes items calling for performance with highly improbable givens are created solely to keep the instructor amused. After all, it can get rather boring to test students over and over with items that are reasonable and practical. But the result of all this is that the instructor doesn't learn how well students are likely to do that which is expected of them. (The instructor also gains a well-deserved reputation for capriciousness, arbitrariness, unprofessionalism, and maybe even stupidity among his/her students.) In this case the rule of reason says:

When a range of stimuli and/or conditions is to be used in a series of test items, use only those stimuli and conditions that students will encounter within six months of the time they are tested.

This rule means simply that the items should match the objective in performance and that the givens and conditions should be reasonable. What's reasonable? Well, it's reasonable to prepare students to handle situations they will run into within the immediate future. It is not reasonable to insist that they be able to handle situations that are known to be highly improbable. There is nothing magical about six months; it is merely a guide. If, in your situation, three or nine months make more sense, then that is the guide to use. If you are an expert in your subject, you will either know what is and is not probable, or you can find out. If you can't find out, then don't write test items.

Remember, there's no test that will guarantee that the skill needed to handle a rarely occurring situation will still be there when needed, because unused skills deteriorate. They leak away—in short, they atrophy. So if it is important that students be able to handle a situation that may occur only rarely, and if the consequence is dire (e.g., "If you don't push the panic button as soon as the red light comes on, the sky will fall."), then give them refresher training often enough to warrant confidence that the skill will be there if needed.

Item Difficulty

It has been common practice to try to arrange the difficulty of a test item so that just about half the students get it right. Difficulty indices are often computed for each item, on the grounds that an item must not be too easy or too hard.

This is a norm-referenced practice and has nothing to do with the practice of finding out if objectives have been achieved. The practice is perfectly defensible when one wants to know how well a given student can perform in relation to his or her peers or when testing the *extent* of someone's content knowledge in a given area. But when you want to know *whether or not* people can do something you want them to do, what's the sense of being arbitrarily devious by making items easier or harder? Ask them simply and directly to do the thing you are after.

The expression "the item was too easy" implies a terrible thing about the nature of education. It implies that rather than work to help as many students as possible to achieve important objectives, many educators act instead to *limit* the amount of instructional success they will tolerate. It implies that if too many students are able to perform as desired, rather than jump up and down with joy at such success, many educators will arbitrarily make the test more difficult.

> "Everybody accomplished all the objectives, so I'm going to have to make the test harder."

Unfortunately, there is substance to these implications. Education is *not* yet designed to be totally successful; many educators do limit the amount of success they will allow. As mentioned earlier, the use of the normal curve is evidence of such limitation. No matter how well the students perform, no matter how many meet or exceed the instructor's expectations, only a portion of them will be allowed to think of themselves as competent. Conversely, no matter how poorly a group of students performs, those who perform the best will be given a label (grade) signifying success.

There is further evidence to support the allegation that education is not designed to tolerate total success. Ask yourself and your colleagues what would happen to them if their instruction *were* totally successful and that, as a result, they gave every student an A and could prove the grades were deserved. Would this result in a banquet in their honor? Applause from their peers? A raise from the administration? Seldom. Though there are now a few institutions that will tolerate total instructional success, the majority still seem bent on fulfilling the prophecy of the "normal" curve.

The message is this: don't worry about item difficulty. Make the items clear and make them match the objective. If everyone performs perfectly, shout with joy. Or with Mary, if you prefer. But in any case, rejoice.

Grading

Another question that often oozes to the surface has to do with that weird practice called grading. The issue shows itself in a variety of forms.

"But if all the students get it right, how can I give grades?"

"If the items are too easy, everybody will get them right."

"Gee, I'm not allowed to give everybody an A, no matter how well they can perform. It just isn't done."

"What about the students who try hard but don't quite make the criterion? Surely you don't expect me to fail them?"

"What about the students who do ten times more than I ask for—surely I can't give them the same grade as the ones who just barely squeak through?"

Each of these sentiments arises from a concern caused by the shift from the old norm-referenced way of grading to the criterion-referenced method of grading. It used to be acceptable to grade students by comparing them with one another. It didn't seem to matter whether the best students could actually do what instructors wanted them to be able to do; if they were better at something than anyone else in the class, they got the highest grades.

"Nobody in this class accomplished any of the objectives, but since Jack and Jill didn't accomplish them with the most style, I'm going to give them each an A."
Or . . .

"Make sure that some of our products are defective when they leave the factory. I don't want to be known as a manager who runs a 'Mickey Mouse' operation because all the products work perfectly."

The practice of giving the "best-in-class" the highest grades can lead to dire consequences. Imagine you are flying along in a jumbo jet when the pilot announces, "Ladies and gentlemen, we are about to begin our descent. There is absolutely nothing to worry about." And then adds, condescendingly, "I got perfect scores on almost all my exams . . . I only flunked landing."

(The Nuclear Regulatory Commission requires nuclear-power-plant operators to get 80% right on multiple-choice exams to be certified. Does that make you feel secure?)

The norm-referenced system is simply not appropriate when you have important objectives for students to achieve. Regardless of how hard students try, or how close they are to reaching competence, if they *can't* perform they *mustn't* be certified as being able to perform. You'll want to know *why* a student failed to achieve an objective, of course, so you can provide the necessary instruction and practice. But until that student *can* perform, you shouldn't pretend that he or she can.

And when you discover that all your students can perform according to the objectives, should they not be certified as being able to perform as desired?

"Oh, but I couldn't give everybody an A," is a comment often heard. But why not? If an A means that a student is able to perform each of the objectives, why would you not be willing to certify that he or she can perform? What does it mean to say you are "not allowed to give everybody an A"? If it means that your institution or school system isn't designed to cope with that much success, then some serious changes are in order. If it means that there would be adverse consequences to you because too many of your students were successful, then again, some serious changes are in order, because the implication is that your job is to produce failures. And that's obscene. Whenever the normal curve is used as a basis for grading, the user is legislating *in advance* the amount of success he or she will tolerate. With the curve system, one is saying to the students, "It doesn't matter how well you can perform . . . only a certain percentage of you will be allowed to think of yourselves as successful" (i.e., we'll only admit that a certain percentage of you are any good).

Some schools have adopted a pass-fail grading arrangement. But what does *pass* mean? Without well-stated objectives, nobody knows. In some courses it means that a minimum score on an exam has been made. In others, that attendance was adequate. In still others it means that students have completed all the assignments. But "pass" is little better than a letter grade unless the nature and the number of the objectives that are represented by the pass or the grade are made public.

A more meaningful reporting system lists the competencies accomplished by individual students. Such a list, in effect, says, "These are the things this student can do," and is a much better indicator of achievement than either a letter grade or a "pass."

"Affective" Objectives

You may have noticed that all the examples used so far have dealt with knowing and doing performances. Nothing whatever has been said about "affective" objectives (those that describe feeling states). That's because there is no such thing as an "affective objective." That's an oxymoron—a contradiction in terms. By the time you have described what students will have to do to convince you that an "affective" state has been accomplished, those descriptions will be written in performance terms and thus can be turned into objectives. And if they are objectives, they won't include "affective" words. Though the objectives may have been derived from definitions of affective states, they won't look any different than other objectives.

There is no question that issues such as attitudes, motivation, growth, and development are important. You should indeed concern yourselves with how students feel about the instruction you offer them and about their values and aspirations. But statements that describe abstract states or intentions (e.g., "Be able to value free enterprise" and "Have a love of learning") contain no "doing" words and so are not objectives. You can't match test items to statements that don't include performances.

If you have a special interest in the "affective" area, I'd like to refer you to two small books that address this topic in some detail.[2]

What Next?

The next chapter offers some guided practice. If you don't feel the need for more practice, then go directly to the skill check of Chapter 8, called "Got a Match?" Your choice.

I'd like a little practice.   **page 111**

I'm ready to test my skill.   **page 145**

2. Read *How to Turn Learners On ... without turning them off*, Third Edition, R. F. Mager; and *Goal Analysis*, Third Edition, R.F. Mager. Copyrights © 2012, Mager Associates, Inc.

7
A Pride of Items

A common instructional error is to send students away without their having had practice doing that which is the object of the instruction. A widely practiced variation is that of giving students practice in performing as desired and then testing more complex concepts and skills than were practiced. Not wishing to be guilty of such deviousness, I present in this chapter some optional exercises containing the same kinds of items you will find on the skill check (criterion test) in Chapter 8. Keep the removable Objective/Item Matching Checklist card handy as you proceed (it's located between the last page and the back cover of this book); it will remind you of the key steps of the matching procedure.

Three kinds of practice will be presented, followed by information with which you can check your own responses.

1. *Yes or no.* Each practice item will consist of an objective and a criterion item. Your task will be to say whether the item is appropriate for assessing achievement of the objective. While you may rightly feel that *several* items would be needed to determine if the objective has been accomplished, you will be asked only to say whether the presented item matches the objective.

2. *Which, if any.* Each practice item will consist of an objective and a series of items, each allegedly appropriate for

assessing achievement of the objective. Your task will be to review each item and say whether it is or is not appropriate for testing the objective.

3. *Fix it.* Each practice item will consist of an objective and an allegedly appropriate item. But something will be wrong. Either the objective will need some repair, or for some reason the item won't match. Your task will be to repair things so that the item will be satisfactory as a test of the objective. If you apply the step-by-step procedure for checking the appropriateness of an item, you shouldn't have any trouble.

"Wait a minute," I hear you screaming. "How come the objective of the book asks me to be able to identify items that match objectives, and now you want me to do a repair job?" And a very astute question that is. You're right, of course; the objective is for you to be able to recognize test items that do or don't match an objective, and that is exactly what you will be asked to do in Chapter 8. By asking you to repair a few objectives and/or items, however, you will be more likely to attend closely to the critical characteristics of each. But the fixing is just for practice; it wouldn't be correct to ask you to fix objectives and items on the skill check merely because it was "covered" in the instruction. In Chapter 8, you will only find items that match the objective of the book.

Working Through the Matching Task

One of the testers of the draft manuscript suggested that before sending readers off to practice the entire matching procedure, another example or two showing how I work through the matching task would be helpful. So I'll show you an objective and an item and then offer the stream of thought that ekes forth as I work my way through the matching process.

Example 1

Objective: *Given a group of numerical expressions, be able to circle examples of the commutative property of addition.*

Criterion Item: *Underline the numerical expressions that are examples of the commutative property of addition.*

$$(a)\ 3 + 7 = 2 + 8 \qquad (d)\ 5 + 2 = 2 + 5$$

$$(b)\ 4 + 5 = 5 + 4 \qquad (e)\ 9 + 1 = 5 + 5$$

$$(c)\ 0 + 4 = 4 + 0 \qquad (f)\ 6 + 2 = 2 + 6$$

Thoughts While Matching. I'll begin with the objective. What's the performance called for in the objective? "Circle examples." I'll circle it so it won't escape. Now what's the main intent? Well, the objective wants students to be able to recognize examples of the commutative property (whatever that is) when they see them. That means the stated performance (circling) is an indicator. Is it the simplest, most direct indicator I can think of? Not bad. Circling is easy to do and the quality of the circling is not likely to be confused with the quality of the recognizing. Is circling well within the repertoire of the students? I can't tell for sure unless I know exactly who the target audience is, but unless it is a group that doesn't know how to, or cannot, use a pencil, the indicator should be just fine.

Now for the item. The item wants students to underline numerical expressions. I'll circle that. Do the performances match? Well, circling isn't exactly the same behavior as underlining, but both can be used to indicate whether students can recognize the desired property, and they are both simple and direct. So the performances match.

What about the conditions? The objective says students are to be given some numerical expression to work with, and the item does just that. The objective asks them to indicate examples of the commutative property, and the item does, too. So the item matches the objective and would be useful for finding out if the objective has been achieved.

Example 2

Here's an example of the same process when the objective exists and an item needs to be drafted to test it.

> **Objective:** *At the end of the course, the student should be familiar with the process of joining and splitting given cells in the Spiffy Spreadsheet program, using the Eunuch terminal provided.*

> **Thoughts While Drafting.** Let's begin with the objective. Good grief! That's awful. I can't draft an item until I have a decent objective, so either I'll have to rewrite it or get its author to do it.

> **Objective:** *Given a Eunuch terminal and Spiffy Spreadsheet software, be able to join and split given cells.*

That's better. No criterion, so I'll have to talk with the objective writer. Now then. The performance is to be able to join and split cells. Is that the point of the objective (main intent)? Sure looks like it. So in this case the main intent is visible, and therefore it is its own indicator. So the test item must ask for splitting and joining of spreadsheet cells. What about conditions? Well, the performer will be provided with a terminal and software, as well as with some specific cells to join or split asunder. OK, let's draft an item.

Criterion Item: *Go to Eunuch terminal #3. The terminal has been booted and a Spiffy Spreadsheet file has been opened. Do two things to the spreadsheet:*

> *1. Join cells B23 and C23.*
>
> *2. Split cells A19 and A20.*

Save your changes and ask an instructor to check your work.

There's a draft. The item asks for the same performance as does the objective, under the conditions specified. I'll have the objective writer check this to make sure I haven't distorted the intent of the objective.

You can see that though I appeared not to have followed each of the checklist items in the precise order given, I did ask the relevant questions. And now it's your turn.

Practice Items

YES OR NO

Each item below consists of an objective and a test item. If the item matches the objective—that is, if the item is suitable for testing achievement of the objective—check (✓) the YES column to the right. If the item is not suitable, for whatever reason, check (✓) the NO column.

	A match?
	YES NO

1. *Objective:* Given Sunday comics, be able to list all of the individual strip titles within the classifications of dry humor, light humor, romance, mysteries, detective stories, adventure, sociology, and religion.

   Criterion Item: Name three comic strips that deal with light humor.   _____   _____

2. *Objective:* Be able to list five major pieces of legislation that were passed in the United States during the Progressive Era (1900-1917).

   Criterion Item: Underline five of the following pieces of twentieth-century legislation that were passed during the Progressive Era (1900-1917).

   (a) Pure Food and Drug Act

   (b) Federal Reserve Act

   (c) Underwood Tariff

   (d) Hepburn Act

   (e) Prohibition Act

   (f) Social Security Act   _____   _____

3. *Objective:* Given ten minority groups in the United States, list at least eight of them in order according to total population.

   Criterion Item: What are eight of the largest minority groups in the United States?   _____   _____

Turn to the next page to check your responses.

	A match?	
	YES	**NO**

1. *Objective:* Given Sunday comics, be able to list all of the individual strip titles within the classifications of dry humor, light humor, romance, mysteries, detective stories, adventure, sociology, or religion.

    Criterion Item: Name three comic strips that deal withlight humor.   _____ ✓

2. *Objective:* Be able to list five major pieces of legislation that were passed in the United States during the Progressive Era (1900-1917).

    Criterion Item: Underline five of the following pieces of twentieth-century legislation that were passed during the Progressive Era (1900-1917).

    (a) Pure Food and Drug Act

    (b) Federal Reserve Act

    (c) Underwood Tariff

    (d) Hepburn Act

    (e) Prohibition Act

    (f) Social Security Act   _____ ✓

3. *Objective:* Given ten minority groups in the United States, list at least eight of them in order according to total population.

    Criterion Item: What are eight of the largest minority groups in the United States?   _____ ✓

1. No match. The objective asks the student to list (main intent is recall); the test item also asks the student to recall, but to recall something different from the demands of the objective. So the performances don't match.

    The objective provides the student with comic strips to review; the test item does not, so the conditions don't match.

2. No match. The objective says list (recall) and the item says underline (recognize).

3. No match. The performances don't match. The objective says the learner will be given something and he or she is to rearrange them. The item asks the learner to recall. Moreover, the objective asks for an arrangement in order according to population; the item only asks for a list of the largest. The item therefore tests for something different than does the objective.

More Practice Items

A match?

	YES	NO

4. *Objective:* Given the original price and the sale price of an article, be able to compute the rate of discount of the article to the nearest whole percent.

   Criterion Item: A boat normally selling for $1,500 is on sale for $1,200. What is the rate of discount to the nearest whole percent?　　　_____　_____

5. *Objective:* Be able to perform a neurological examination using proper techniques and equipment.

   Criterion Item: Describe the equipment and procedures used to conduct a neurological examination.　　　_____　_____

6. *Objective:* For each of these procedures (craniotomy, laminectomy), describe the locations and functions of the scrub nurse and assistants.

   Criterion Item: Describe the locations and functions of the scrub nurse and assistants for each of these surgical procedures:

   (a) Craniotomy

   (b) Laminectomy　　　_____　_____

7. *Objective:* Having written a broad intent (goal) you feel worthy of achievement, be able to list the performances which, if achieved, will cause you to agree that the goal is also achieved. (That is, write the operational definition of a goal you consider worthy of achievement.)

   Criterion Item: Which of the following goals do you feel is most worthy of achievement in today's society?

   (a) Good citizenship

   (b) Population reduction

   (c) Law and order

   (d) Honest government

8. *Objective:* Be able to list four possible elements of kidnapping that are outlined in the Penal Code, Section 208.

   Criterion Item: Joe has taken Tom across the state line against his will. Which section of the Penal Code outlines this action as a kidnapping?

Refer to the next few pages to check your responses.

	A match?	
	YES	**NO**

4. *Objective:* Given the original price and the sale price of an article, be able to compute the rate of discount of the article to the nearest whole percent.

   Criterion Item: A boat normally selling for $1,500 is on sale for $1,200. What is the rate of discount to the nearest whole percent?   ✓   ____

5. *Objective:* Be able to perform a neurological examination using proper techniques and equipment.

   Criterion Item: Describe the equipment and procedures used to conduct a neurological examination.   ____   ✓

6. *Objective:* For each of these procedures (craniotomy, laminectomy), describe the locations and functions of the scrub nurse and assistants.

   Criterion Item: Describe the locations and functions of the scrub nurse and assistants for each of these surgical procedures:

   (a) Craniotomy

   (b) Laminectomy   ✓   ____

4. A match. Both objective and item ask the student to find the rate of discount, and the item asks for that performance under the same conditions described by the objective. Additional items might be used in a complete performance test, of course, but each would need to be of this type.

5. Not on your life. Describing equipment and procedures is not at all the same as performing an examination. No match.

6. A match. The item matches the objective in every way. Notice that you didn't have to be big in medical knowledge to tell whether the item matches the objective. This isn't always true, but it should be comforting to know that you can spot good or bad items in fields other than your own.

A match?

	YES	NO

7. *Objective:* Having written a broad intent (goal) you feel worthy of achievement, be able to list the performances which, if achieved, will cause you to agree that the goal is also achieved. (That is, write the operational definition of a goal you consider worthy of achievement.)

   Criterion Item: Which of the following goals do you feel is most worthy of achievement in today's society?

   (a) Good citizenship

   (b) Population reduction

   (c) Law and order

   (d) Honest government   _____ ✓_____

8. *Objective:* Be able to list four possible elements of kidnapping that are outlined in the Penal Code, Section 208.

   Criterion Item: Joe has taken Tom across the state line against his will. Which section of the Penal Code outlines this action as a kidnapping?   _____ ✓_____

7. No match. The objective calls for deriving a list of performances, and that appears to be the main intent. The item clearly does not ask for the same thing. To be suitable, the item would have to ask the student to derive a list of performances that define a goal. No other type of item form would suffice.

8. No match. The objective says to list (recall) four elements. The item offers a situation and asks the student to recall a section that applies.

More Practice Items

WHICH, IF ANY

Following are three objectives and a set of test items for each. If an item matches the objective, check the YES column to the right. If not, check the NO column.

Is the item appropriate?

	YES	NO

Objective #1: Be able to construct a parallelogram of any given dimensions that is accurate to within 1.5 cm.

Test Items:

1. Define parallelogram.   ____   ____

2. Describe the difference between a parallelogram and a rectangle.   ____   ____

3. Look at the following figures and draw a circle around the one that is a parallelogram.   ____   ____

4. Draw a parallelogram whose sides are 11 cm and 13 cm in length.   ____   ____

5. Construct a parallelogram whose sides are 5 cm and 7 cm in length, accurate to ± 1.5 cm.   ____   ____

Turn the page to check your responses.

| | **Is the item appropriate?** | |
	YES	**NO**

Objective #1: Be able to construct a parallelogram of any given dimensions that is accurate to within 1.5 cm.

Test Items:

1. Define parallelogram. | | ✓

2. Describe the difference between a parallelogram and a rectangle. | | ✓

3. Look at the following figures and draw a circle around the one that is a parallelogram. | | ✓

4. Draw a parallelogram whose sides are 11 cm and 13 cm in length. | ✓ | (?)

5. Construct a parallelogram whose sides are 5 cm and 7 cm in length, accurate to ± 1.5 cm. | ✓ |

1. One of the least appropriate items imaginable (though popu-
   lar). "But students don't really understand parallelograms
   unless they can define one," one might cry in anguish. All right.
   But if you feel that way about it, either teach your students the
   definition as enrichment or background and don't test on it, or
   write an objective that reflects your intent.

2. No match. This item might be useful for finding out why a
   student has *not* achieved the objective—but it is not appropriate for finding out if he or she *has* achieved it.

3. Not appropriate. Again, this item might be good for discover-
   ing that students had not achieved the objective because they
   couldn't recognize a parallelogram when they saw one, but it
   won't tell whether they can construct one.

4. Well, if you are non-mathematical like me, this item would be
   okay. A mathematician, however, makes a distinction
   between drawing and constructing. Drawing is what one does
   when sketching freehand; constructing is what one does
   when drawing accurately with the use of instruments.

5. Appropriate. Finally. Use as many such items as you feel are
   necessary to sample the stimulus range, ensuring that each
   item asks students to construct a parallelogram.

More Practice Items

Objective #2: Be able to read a domestic electric-power meter correctly to the nearest unit, and record your readings on the appropriate page of the meter reader's log.

Test Items:

1. Record on the appropriate page of your log the readings of each of these ten domestic meters to the nearest unit.   _____ _____

2. Of the five dials on the domestic meter, which records "thousands of units"?   _____ _____

3. Look at this picture of a dial. What is the reading?   _____ _____

4. Look at the dials on these domestic meters. What are the readings?   _____ _____

5. Define kilowatt-hour.   _____ _____

Turn the page to check your responses.

	Is the item appropriate?	
	YES	NO

Objective #2: Be able to read a domestic electric-power meter correctly to the nearest unit, and record your readings on the appropriate page of the meter reader's log.

Test Items:

1. Record on the appropriate page of your log the readings of each of these ten domestic meters to the nearest unit.   ✓   ____   ____

2. Of the five dials on the domestic meter, which records "thousands of units"?   ____   ✓   ____

3. Look at this picture of a dial. What is the reading?   ____   ✓   ____

4. Look at the dials on these domestic meters. What are the readings?   ____   ✓   ____

5. Define kilowatt-hour.   ____   ✓   ____

1. An appropriate item. The objective says "read and record" to the nearest unit, and the test item says "record" to the nearest unit. Presumably meter readers can't record what they haven't read, so I would consider this item a match. If you think I am assuming too much, then a small modification of the test item would be in order.

2. This might be a good diagnostic item and useful for determining whether a person who had not achieved the objective was having trouble because he or she didn't know which dial was showing what, but it is not adequate for finding out whether one can read and record complete readings in a book.

3. This one tests for *part* of the objective, to be sure, but not for the entire objective. You may learn that a person can read the dials properly, but you won't find out if he or she can read and then record to the nearest unit.

4. Same problem as Item 3. If an item is not appropriate for testing achievement of an objective, adding several more items of the same type will not improve matters.

5. Not appropriate. What is the main intent of the objective? Read and record. What does the test item ask for? A definition. They are not the same.

More Practice Items

This one is a little more subtle than it may appear. Follow the checklist and you shouldn't have any trouble.

	Is the item appropriate?	
	YES	**NO**

Objective #3: Be able to type a business letter in accordance with the standards described in Company Manual 12-21.

Test Items:

1. Describe the five basic elements of a business letter.	____	____
2. Sort the ten sample letters into piles representing those that are written in accordance with Company standards and those that are not.	____	____
3. On the five sample letters given, circle any errors or items not in accordance with standards of good grammar.	____	____
4. Describe in a paragraph the rationale for the business letter standards currently in effect.	____	____
5. From the handwritten copy given, type a business letter in the form set out by manual 12-21.	____	____

Turn the page to check your responses.

	Is the item appropriate?	
	YES	NO

Objective #3: Be able to type a business letter in accordance with the standards described in Company Manual 12-21.

Test Items:

1. Describe the five basic elements of a business letter.   _____ ✓

2. Sort the ten sample letters into piles representing those that are written in accordance with Company standards and those that are not.   _____ ✓

3. On the five sample letters given, circle any errors or items not in accordance with standards of good grammar.   _____ ✓

4. Describe in a paragraph the rationale for the business letter standards currently in effect.   _____ ✓

5. From the handwritten copy given, type a business letter in the form set out by manual 12-21.   _____ ✓

1. The objective says *type,* and the test items says *describe.* Not the same, so you needn't even bother to look at the conditions.

2. Not appropriate. Typing is not the same as sorting. During instruction, sorting might be a useful activity to sharpen the ability to recognize letters written according to company standards. Or, it might be a good diagnostic item for finding out why a student *cannot* type letters as desired. But it is not appropriate for testing achievement of the objective.

3. Not appropriate. Same comment as for Item 2.

4. Neither the performance nor the conditions match. (To chant "I like to vary the type of test items I use to make my tests more interesting" doesn't make this item any more acceptable.)

5. Here's the sticky one. The performances match. Right? Both objective and item ask students to type a letter. So far, so good. But the test item asks for typing under conditions *different* from those called for by the objective, i.e., typing from *handwritten* copy. If you don't type much, this point could easily slip by; but typists know that it can be very difficult to have to type from scraggly handwritten copy. The objective or the item needs to be changed to match the other.

More Practice Items

FIX IT

Below are pairs of statements, each pair consisting of an objective and a test item allegedly appropriate for testing whether the objective has been achieved. Edit (fix, repair) either the objective, the item, or both, so that there is a match.

1. **Objective:** Given a recipe, all necessary utensils, and ingredients, be able to bake a cherry pie. Criteria: (a) the crust is brown but not burned, (b) the cherry juice has not run out of the pie, and (c) the instructor did not die immediately after tasting it.

   Test Item: Following is a recipe for cherry pie. In the space below, describe (write) the steps you would follow in baking a cherry pie.

2. **Objective:** Be able to describe to a customer the primary services provided by the bank.

   Test Item: Circle the services that are available to bank customers.

   (a) Checking accounts   (d) Manicures

   (b) Savings accounts   (e) Loans

   (c) Neck massages   (f) Mortgages

Check your fixes on the next page.

1. **Objective:** Given a recipe, all necessary utensils, and ingredients, be able to bake a cherry pie. Criteria: (a) The crust is brown but not burned, (b) the cherry juice has not run out of the pie, and (c) the instructor did not die immediately after tasting it.

   Test Item: Following is a recipe for cherry pie. In the space below, describe (write) the steps you would follow in baking a cherry pie.

   This one is easy. The main intent of the objective is to bake a cherry pie. The item asks someone to describe the steps. Baking and describing are not the same, so something has to change. If we assume that the objective is correct, then we have to make the item match. Something like this:

   Objective: *Given a recipe, all necessary utensils, and ingredients, be able to bake a cherry pie. Criteria: (a) the crust is brown but not burned, (b) the cherry juice has not run out of the pie, and (c) the instructor did not die immediately after tasting it.*

   Test Item: *Go to Cookspace #3, where you will find a recipe for cherry pie, along with all the utensils and ingredients you will need. Bake a cherry pie. Your finished pie will be accepted when it is determined that the crust is brown but not burned, the juice didn't run out, and it didn't immediately kill the instructor who tasted it.*

2. **Objective:** Be able to describe to a customer the primary services provided by the bank.

   Test Item: Circle the services that are available to bank customers.

   (a) Checking accounts   (d) Manicures

   (b) Savings accounts   (e) Loans

   (c) Neck massages   (f) Mortgages

Here you'll need to match performances; the objective asks for a verbal performance (describe to a customer), and the item merely asks for recognition (identify by circling). I would make the objective and item read as follows, though your own version is acceptable if the performances and conditions match.

Objective: *Using the list of services provided, be able to describe verbally each of the bank services that is available to the customer. For each service, present the following information: (a) what the service is and what it provides, (b) how the service may be obtained, and (c) the cost of the service to the customer.*

Test Item: *Using the tape recorder provided and a list of bank services, record your description of each service. Include in each description (a) the extent of the service, (b) information on how it may be obtained, and (c) cost.*

More Practice Items

FIX ONE MORE

3. *Objective:* Given a functioning computer terminal and a word processing program with which you are familiar, be able to draft and print a business memo. Criterion: The memo meets the standards described on pp. 45-46 in the Corporate Policy Manual.

   Test Item: Draft a business memo on a topic of your choice. The memo should conform to the Corporate Policy Manual, pp. 45-46. Use your own terminal and the word processing software of your choice.

Turn the page to check your revision.

3. **Objective:** *Given a functioning computer terminal and a word processing program with which you are familiar, be able to draft and print a business memo. Criterion: The memo meets the standards described on pp. 45-46 in the Corporate Policy Manual.*

Test Item: *Draft a business memo on a topic of your choice. The memo should conform to the Corporate Policy Manual, pp. 45-46. Use your own terminal and the word processing software of your choice.*

This pair is pretty good. Both call for the same performance (writing a business memo). The objective, however, calls for a printed memo and the item doesn't. One or the other has to be changed. If you change the item, it might look like this:

Test Item: *Draft a business memo on a topic of your choice, and print out a hard copy of the memo. The memo should conform to the Corporate Policy Manual, pp. 45-46. Use your own terminal and the word processing software of your choice.*

That should be enough practice to enable you to whiz through the skill check (Chapter 8) in blazing glory. Have at it.

8
Got a Match?

It's time to discover whether you are able to recognize criterion (test) items suitable for assessing achievement of an objective. How shall this be done? Shall I ask you to trace the history of testing or to write an essay on the significance of the multiple-choice item? Mmmm. I've got it! I'll write an item that asks you to compare and contrast norm-referenced with criterion-referenced testing. If you can do that, I can conclude that you really understand the subject. Right?

Oh. I can see you're going to be fussy about it, so I'd better try to practice what I've been trying to get you to practice. On the other hand, the temptation is great to slip in a few items that test the limits or breadth of your understanding. You know how it is—if I just use items that test for the objective, you might get them all correct. And then where would I be? I'd have to write some "harder" items so you didn't get the idea the "course" was too easy. Right? All right, enough is enough, but I just couldn't resist one last chance to make the point that it isn't exactly being honest with students to tell them you want them to be able to do one thing and then test their ability to do something else.

So let's get on with it. Here are some criterion items, each of which is appropriate for testing the objective of this book which is, you'll recall:

Be able to discriminate (select, point to) test items that are appropriate for testing the achievement of an instructional objective, when given

    (a) An objective

    (b) One or more allegedly suitable test items

    (c) The Objective/Item Matching Checklist

Section I. Yes, No, or Can't Tell

The following 10 pairs of statements each consist of an objective and a test item. If the test item is appropriate for testing achievement of the objective, check the YES column to the right. If the item is not appropriate, check the NO column. If you can't apply the matching procedure because the objective is too fuzzy (i.e., doesn't state a performance), check the CAN'T TELL column.

Is the item suitable?

YES   NO   CAN'T TELL

---

1. *Objective:* Given a performance of an instrumental or vocal melody containing a melodic or rhythmic error, and given the score for the melody, be able to point out the error.

    Criterion Item: The instructor will play the melody of the attached musical score on the piano and will make an error either in rhythm or melody. Raise your hand when the error occurs.

(continued on next page)

Is the item suitable?
YES   NO   CAN'T
TELL

2. *Objective:* Given mathematical equations containing one unknown, be able to solve for the unknown.

    Criterion Item: Sam weighs 97 kilos. He weighs 3.5 kilos more than Barney. How much does Barney weigh?   ____   ____   ____

3. *Objective:* Be able to demonstrate familiarity with sexual anatomy and physiology.

    Criterion Item: Draw and label a sketch of the male and female reproductive systems.   ____   ____   ____

4. *Objective:* Given any one of the computers in our product line, in its original carton, be able to install and adjust the machine, preparing it for use.

    Criteria: The machine shows normal indication, and the area is free of debris and cartons.

    Criterion Item: Select one of the cartons containing one of our Model XX computers, and install it for the secretary in Room 45. Make sure it is ready for use and the area is left clean.   ____   ____   ____

(continued on next page)

Is the item suitable?
YES NO CAN'T
TELL

5. *Objective:* When given a set of paragraphs (that use words within your vocabulary), some of which are missing topic sentences, be able to identify the paragraphs without topic sentences.

    Criterion Item: Turn to page 29 in your copy of *Silas Marner*. Underline the topic sentence of each paragraph on that page.   —— —— ——

6. *Note:* Not every objective comes in a single sentence. Many objectives that describe a complex or higher-order skill need several sentences, as the following one illustrates. Use your checklist, and the objective should fall easily into place.

    Objective: Given a chapter in a textbook, be able to derive and draw a hierarchy of the objectives accomplished by the chapter. Each objective must state the action required of the student and any important conditions under which the action is to be performed.

    Criteria need not be specified. The pyramid should extend through at least two levels of subordinate objectives or to the assumed entry-level skills of the target population, whichever chain is longer.

(continued on next page)

Is the item suitable?
YES NO CAN'T
TELL

Criterion Item: Refer to Chapter 7 in the textbook, *Nuclear Physics for Fun and Profit.* Derive and state the objectives actually accomplished by the chapter, and then draw a hierarchy of the objectives. Each objective must state the action required of the student and any important conditions under which the action is to be performed. Criteria need not be specified. The pyramid should extend through two levels of subordinate objectives or to the assumed entry-level skills of the target population, whichever chain is longer.

____ ____ ____

7. *Objective:* Given live or video demonstrations of various actions, be able to tell which actions are in violation of Section 415, Disturbing the Peace.

   Criterion Item: Check each of the following actions that represent a violation of Section 415, Disturbing the Peace.

   (a) Helen fires a pistol into the ground in her own back yard.

   (b) Hal and Joe are having a fistfight in the corner bar.

   (c) Sarah, wanting to sleep, asks her neighbor to turn down a noisy TV. The neighbor turns it up to full volume.

____ ____ ____

(continued on next page)

Is the item suitable?
YES   NO   CAN'T
TELL

8. *Objective:* Be able to taxi any C-series aircraft, according to criteria stated in the Flight Crew Checklist, without performing steps that are unnecessary or a danger to the aircraft, its crew, or other aircraft in the area.

   Criterion Item: Following is a list of steps to be completed before taxi of the C-124A aircraft. Check (✓) those that are correct, and "X" those that are unnecessary or incorrect.

   ___ (a) Hydraulic pressure "WITHIN LIMITS"

   ___ (b) Brakes "CHECKED"

   ___ (c) Flight instruments "CO-PILOT'S CHECKED" (CP), "PILOT'S CHECKED" (S)

   ___ (d) Scanner's report "ENGINE CHECKED" (S)

   ___ (e) CHECK COMPLETED (CP)   ___ ___ ___

9. *Objective:* Be able to observe any patient and tell which of the patient's characteristics should be responded to and which should be ignored (i.e., not responded to).

   Criterion Item: Describe to your instructor any five patient characteristics that should be responded to and at least five characteristics from which you should withhold a response.   ___ ___ ___

(continued on next page)

Is the item suitable?
YES   NO   CAN'T
TELL

10. *Objective:* Given a Model 31 Brain-wash-
er, a standard tool kit, a standard spares
kit, test equipment, and at least one symptom of a common malfunction, be able to
return the system to normal operation.

Criteria: The system functions within
specifications. There is no cosmetic or
structural damage to the system or to the
immediate area. No more than one
unnecessary spare part is used. All paperwork is completed correctly, and no complaints are filed by client personnel.

Criterion Item: The model 31 Brainwasher in the test room can be turned on,
but the washing fluid leaks onto the
brain-removal mechanism during the
wash cycle. Return the machine to normal
operating condition. The tool kit, spares,
and test equipment beside the machine
are available as you need them. Call the
instructor when you have finished.

Section II. Which, If Any

Following are four objectives and a set of test items for each. If an item is appropriate for testing the objective, check the YES column at the right. If not, check the NO column. If an item is in some way obscure so that you can't apply the matching procedure, check the CAN'T TELL column.

Is the item suitable?
YES   NO   CAN'T
TELL

A. *Objective:* When approached by a prospective customer, be able to respond in a positive manner (with a smile, a suitable greeting, and a pleasant tone of voice).

Criterion Items:

1. Describe the three basic characteristics of a positive response to the approach of a prospective customer.

2. Watch the following ten film clips and write down the numbers of those that represent a correct response to the approach of a prospective customer.

3. When the instructor hangs the "customer" sign around his neck and approaches you, make the positive response to the approach of a prospective customer.

4. When approached by each of five students selected by the instructor, make the appropriate (positive) response to customer approach.

Is the item suitable?
YES   NO   CAN'T
                    TELL

B. *Objective:* Given the stock-market quotations from recent news-papers for two different dates and a schedule of brokerage fees, be able to compute the profit or loss resulting from the "buy" of a given number of shares on the earliest of the two dates and a "sell" on the latest.

Criterion Items:

1. In Packet A are stock-market quotations from newspapers of different days and a schedule of brokerage fees. For each of the five stocks circled, calculate the profit or loss that would result from buying 12 shares of the stock on the earlier date and selling them on the later date. Write the profit or loss in the spaces provided.   ＿＿ ＿＿ ＿＿

2. In Packet A are stock-market quotations from newspapers of different days and a schedule of brokerage fees. Describe in writing how brokerage fees are applied to any stock sale.   ＿＿ ＿＿ ＿＿

3. Using the schedule of brokerage fees pro-vided, write an example to illustrate how profit and loss are computed for sale of stocks.   ＿＿ ＿＿ ＿＿

4. Explain the meaning of each of the entries shown for the stock circled on the newspa-per stock pages attached.   ＿＿ ＿＿ ＿＿

5. Describe the procedure for buying and sell-ing a stock.   ＿＿ ＿＿ ＿＿

Is the item suitable?
YES   NO   CAN'T
                  TELL

C. *Objective:* Given a malfunctioning amplifier of any design, one symptom, reference materials, and tools, be able to repair the unit so that it functions within design specifications.

Criterion Items:

1. Design an amplifier that meets the specifications shown on the attached sheet. Show the values and tolerances for each component.   ____ ____ ____

2. List the three most common troubles to be expected from each of the amplifier designs contained in Packet A.   ____ ____ ____

3. Attached to this sheet are the schematic diagrams for three different kinds of amplifiers. A red circle is drawn around one component of each amplifier. On the bottom of the page, write the symptom(s) that would show up if the circled components were malfunctioning.   ____ ____ ____

4. At Stations A, B, and C are three amplifiers. The tag on each amplifier describes one symptom of the trouble that has been inserted. Using the tools and references provided at each station, repair each amplifier.   ____ ____ ____

5. At Stations A, B, and C are three amplifiers. The tag on each amplifier describes one symptom of trouble that has been inserted. On the page provided, describe the steps you would take to clear the trouble and put the amplifier back into operation.   ____ ____ ____

Is the item suitable?
YES   NO   CAN'T
TELL

D. *Objective:* Given a set of diagrams or slides of correctly angled periodontal probe calibrations, write the correct probe reading of each, rounded to the next highest millimeter.

Criterion Items:

1. On a periodontal probe, which marks are missing?   ____   ____   ____

2. Look at the slides in Envelope D, and write down the probe reading shown in each. Round your answer to the next highest millimeter.   ____   ____   ____

3. In Envelope E are slides showing probes that have been inserted into the sulcus. For each slide, tell whether any precautions have been overlooked, and if so, which ones.   ____   ____   ____

RESPONSES

Here is how I would respond to the items on the previous pages. Perhaps you would like to compare your responses with mine.

Turn to the next page.

Responses to Section I. Yes, No, or Can't Tell

	Is the item suitable?		
	YES	NO	CAN'T TELL

---

1. *Objective:* Given a performance of an instrumental or vocal melody containing a melodic or rhythmic error, and given the score for the melody, be able to point out the error.

   Criterion Item: The instructor will play the melody of the attached musical score on the piano and will make an error either in rhythm or melody. Raise your hand when the error occurs. ✓ ___ ___

2. *Objective:* Given mathematical equations containing one unknown, be able to solve for the unknown.

   Criterion Item: Sam weighs 97 kilos. He weighs 3.5 kilos more than Barney. How much does Barney weigh? ___ ✓ ___

3. *Objective:* Be able to demonstrate familiarity with sexual anatomy and physiology.

   Criterion Item: Draw and label a sketch of the male and female reproductive systems. ___ ___ ✓

4. *Objective:* Given any one of the computers in our product line, in its original carton, be able to install and adjust the machine, preparing it for use.

   Criteria: The machine shows normal indication, and the area is free of debris and cartons.

   Criterion Item: Select one of the cartons containing one of our Model XX computers, and install it for the secretary in Room 45. Make sure it is ready for use and the area is left clean. ✓ ___ ___

1. The item is suitable. The objective wants students to be able to recognize errors in the performance of a piece of music for which they are given the score; it wants them to detect (*discriminate, locate, spot*) errors between the rendition and the score. The item asks for the same. True, the indicator stated in the objective is "point out," and the test item asks for hand-raising. Since hand-raising is a simple and direct method for indicating the main intent, the item is a match.

2. No match. This one represents a common mismatch between teaching and testing. Students are expected to be able to solve a given type of mathematical equation. Not only does the item not provide an equation to solve, it asks for a different skill. Solving an equation is not the same as setting up an equation from a word problem. Neither the performance nor the conditions match.

3. Can't tell. What is someone doing when demonstrating his or her familiarity with sexual anatomy? Don't answer that! But unless the objective answers it, there is no way to tell if the item is appropriate for checking out success at achievement of the objective.

4. A match. The objective asks someone to install and adjust, as does the test item. The conditions also match.

Is the item suitable?
YES NO CAN'T
TELL

5. *Objective:* When given a set of paragraphs (that use words within your vocabulary), some of which are missing topic sentences, be able to identify the paragraphs without topic sentences.

   Criterion Item: Turn to page 29 in your copy of *Silas Marner.* Underline the topic sentence of each paragraph on that page.   ✓

6. *Objective:* Given a chapter in a textbook, be able to derive and draw a hierarchy of the objectives accomplished by the chapter. Each objective must state the action required of the student and any important conditions under which the action is to be performed. Criteria need not be specified. The hierarchy should extend through at least two levels of subordinate objectives or to the assumed entry-level skills of the target population, whichever chain is longer.

   Criterion Item: Refer to Chapter 7 in the textbook, *Nuclear Physics for Fun and Profit.* Derive and state the objectives actually accomplished by the chapter, and then draw a hierarchy of the objectives. Each objective must state the action required of the student and any important conditions under which the action is to be performed. Criteria need not be specified. The hierarchy should extend through at least two levels of subordinate objectives or to the assumed entry-level skills of the target population, whichever chain is longer.   ✓

5. No match. The objective asks students to identify paragraphs without topic sentences; the item asks them to identify (by underlining) topic sentences. Not the same.

6. A match. The objective asks that learners to able to construct a hierarchy of objectives derived from a chapter in a textbook; the item asks for the same. And though the wording is slightly different between objective and item, the conditions match as well.

   Why does the item look so much like the objective? You know the answer to that. When the performance stated in the objective is mainly overt and at the same time the main intent, there is only one type of item suitable for assessing achievement of the objective—the type that asks learners to do just what the objective says. Only in this instance do the objective and test items look similar; whenever the objective main intent is covert, an indicator must be used, regardless of whether that covert main intent is mainly cognitive or "affective." In those instances the test items look noticeably different from the objective.

Is the item suitable?
YES   NO   CAN'T
TELL

7. *Objective:* Given live or video demon-
    strations of various actions, be able to tell
    which actions are in violation of Section
    415, Disturbing the Peace.

    Criterion Item: Check each of the follow-
    ing actions that represent a violation of
    Section 415, Disturbing the Peace.

    (a) Helen fires a pistol into the
         ground in her own backyard.

    (b) Hal and Joe are having a
         fist fight in the corner bar.

    (c) Sarah, wanting to sleep, asks
         her neighbor to turn down a
         noisy TV. The neighbor turns it   ✓
         up to full volume.   ____ ____ ____

7. No match. Both objective and item want students to be able to identify actions that are violations of Section 415. The objective, however, wants them to be able to do their identifying in response to live or video demonstrations; the item asks for the identifying in response to verbal descriptions of situations. Not the same. If a learner responded well to the item as written, would you be able to conclude that he or she could handle real situations as well? I'm not sure. What is clear is that the item demands an inference about whether the objective has actually been accomplished.

Is the item suitable?
YES NO CAN'T
TELL

---

8. *Objective:* Be able to taxi any C-series aircraft, according to criteria stated in the Flight Crew Checklist, without performing steps that are unnecessary or a danger to the aircraft, its crew, or other aircraft in the area.

   Criterion Item: Following is a list of steps to be completed before taxi of the C-124A aircraft. Check (✓) those that are correct, and "X" those that are unnecessary or incorrect.

   ___ (a) Hydraulic pressure "WITHIN LIMITS"

   ___ (b) Brakes "CHECKED"

   ___ (c) Flight instruments "CO-PILOT'S CHECKED"(CP), "PILOT'S CHECKED" (S)

   ___ (d) Scanner's report "ENGINE CHECKED" (S)

   ___ (e) CHECK COMPLETED (CP)

         ✓

___ ___ ___

8. No match. Taxiing an aircraft and recognizing written steps to be completed before taxiing are not the same.

   Again, the item might be useful as a diagnostic item to reveal one of the reasons the taxiing was not accomplished as desired.

   Or it might be useful as a preflight checkout to find out if a student is ready to try taxiing. After all, you wouldn't let any student taxi an expensive aircraft (they all are) unless you felt confident that he or she knew what to do. But that doesn't slice any bananas. If you want to find out if students can taxi, ask them to taxi.

Is the item suitable?
YES   NO   CAN'T
TELL

9. *Objective:* Be able to observe any patient and tell which of the patient's characteristics should be responded to and which should be ignored (i.e., not responded to).

   Criterion Item: Describe to your instructor any five patient characteristics that should be responded to and at least five characteristics from which you should withhold a response.   ✓   _____ _____ _____

10. *Objective:* Given a Model 31 Brainwasher, a standard tool kit, a standard spares kit, test equipment, and at least one symptom of a common malfunction, be able to return the system to normal operation.

    Criteria: The system functions within specifications. There is no cosmetic or structural damage to the system or to the immediate area. No more than one unnecessary spare part is used. All paperwork is completed correctly, and no complaints are filed by client personnel.

    Criterion Item: The model 31 Brainwasher in the test room can be turned on, but the washing fluid leaks onto the brain-removal mechanism during the wash cycle. Return the machine to normal operating condition. The tool kit, spares, and test equipment beside the machine are available as you need them. Call the instructor when you have finished.   ✓   _____ _____ _____

9. Same as Number 8. Not appropriate. The item asks students to recall some characteristics, while the objective asks them to describe characteristics of real patients. Not the same.

10. Close, but no bell ringer. The performances match, both objective and item ask students to repair a machine when shown at least one symptom of malfunction. And some of the conditions match. But the objective asks that paperwork be completed; the test item asks that the instructor be called when the task is completed. The objective asks that no complaints be filed by client personnel; the test is clearly conducted in a classroom rather than on client premises.

   Of course, it may be necessary or practical (convenient) to do the testing in a classroom instead of on client premises. If that is the case, that wouldn't change the fact that the conditions don't match. If this test item were used as the means of finding out whether the objective was achieved, the evaluators could only infer—make an educated guess—whether the objective was achieved. It might be a pretty good inference about whether a student could repair the machine, but it would be a poor inference about whether a student could work correctly on client premises or complete the necessary paperwork.

Responses to Section II. Which, If Any

Is the item suitable?
YES   NO   CAN'T
TELL

A. *Objective:* When approached by a prospective customer, be able to respond in a positive manner (with a smile, a suitable greeting, and a pleasant tone of voice).

Criterion Items:

1. Describe the three basic characteristics of a positive response to the approach of a prospective customer.   ____ ✓ ____

2. Watch the following ten film clips and write down the numbers of those that represent a correct response to the approach of a prospective customer.   ____ ✓ ____

3. When the instructor hangs the "customer" sign around his neck and approaches you, make the positive response to the approach of a prospective customer.   ✓ ____ ____

4. When approached by each of five students selected by the instructor, make the appropriate (positive) response to customer approach.   ✓ ____ ____

A.

1. No match. Describing characteristics is not the same as responding in a positive manner. Neither performances nor conditions match.

2. No good. Recognizing proper approaches in a film is not the same as responding to a prospective customer. Items 1 and 2 may provide some good practice in developing parts of the desired skill, but they are not useful for finding out if the skill has been developed.

3. Pretty good. The item asks for a response to an instructor who is pretending to be a prospective customer, and so the item is asking for a simulation of the desired performance. Or is it? Maybe the instructor is a prospective customer. You would need to know more about the actual situation to be sure. I would accept this item as suitable, but if you feel the urge to revise it, I will be happy to cheer you on.

4. This one is very similar to the one above, except that it asks for the response to be made five times instead of one and asks that the response be made to students instead of the instructor. The performances match, and the conditions seem very close. If you would not be willing to accept the item, how would you change it?

Is the item suitable?
YES   NO   CAN'T
TELL

B. *Objective:* Given the stock-market quotations from recent newspapers for two different dates and a schedule of brokerage fees, be able to compute the profit or loss resulting from the "buy" of a given number of shares on the earlier of the two dates and a "sell" on the later date.

Criterion Items:

1. In Packet A are stock-market quotations from newspapers of different days and a schedule of brokerage fees. For each of the five stocks circled, calculate the profit or loss that would result from buying 12 shares of the stock on the earlier date and selling them on the later date. Write the profit or loss in the spaces provided.   ✓ ____ ____ ____

2. In Packet A are stock-market quotations from newspapers of different days and a schedule of brokerage fees. Describe in writing how brokerage fees are applied to any stock sale.   ____ ✓ ____

3. Using the schedule of brokerage fees provided, write an example to illustrate how profit and loss is computed for sale of stocks.   ____ ✓ ____

4. Explain the meaning of each of the entries shown for the stock circled on the newspaper stock pages attached.   ____ ✓ ____

5. Describe the procedure for buying and selling a stock.   ____ ✓ ____

B.

1. Item is suitable. The main intent of the objective is that students be able to compute profit and loss on a stock sale. Though the objective doesn't state an indicator, you can safely assume that writing down the result of the calculation is the simplest and most direct indicator that would tell you if the computation is correct. If you don't think you can so assume, I would be happy to support your urge (is that a performance?) to modify the item a little.

2. No good. Describing a procedure is not the same as carrying out the procedure.

3. No good. Writing an example is not the same as calculating profit or loss.

4. Not adequate. But students couldn't calculate profit or loss unless they knew the meaning of the newspaper stock entries, could they? Of course not. But that's not the point, is it? If your intent is for students to be able to describe entries, then that is what the objective should say.

5. Not adequate. Describing a procedure is not the same as carrying out a procedure.

Is the item suitable?
YES   NO   CAN'T
                    TELL

C. *Objective:* Given a malfunctioning amplifier of any design, one symptom, reference materials, and tools, be able to repair the unit so that it functions within design specifications.

Criterion Items:

1. Design an amplifier that meets the specifications shown on the attached sheet. Show the values and tolerances for each component.   ____   ✓   ____

2. List the three most common troubles to be expected from each of the amplifier designs contained in Packet A.   ____   ✓   ____

3. Attached to this sheet are the schematic diagrams for three different kinds of amplifiers. A red circle is drawn around one component of each amplifier. On the bottom of the page, write the symptom(s) that would show up if the circled components were malfunctioning.   ____   ✓   ____

4. At Stations A, B, and C are three amplifiers. The tag on each amplifier describes one symptom of the trouble that has been inserted. Using the tools and references provided at each station, repair each amplifier.   ✓   ____   ____

5. At Stations A, B, and C are three amplifiers. The tag on each amplifier describes one symptom of trouble that has been inserted. On the page provided, describe the steps you would take to clear the trouble and put the amplifier back into operation.   ____   ✓   ____

C.

1. No match. The objective wants students to be able to repair, and the item asks for design. Not the same thing at all. What would you say to someone who said, "But students don't really understand how to fix one unless they can design one"? (Now don't be too nasty.) Hopefully, you would remind that person that while his or her comment has a grain of truth, it is not relevant to the point. If you want to know if learners can fix, ask them to fix.

2. Not adequate. Listing (recalling) common troubles is not the same as repairing an ailing amplifier.

3. Sounds good, but it won't do. Actually, the item is backwards from the objective, in the sense that the objective asks students to go from symptom to trouble, and the item asks them to go from trouble to symptom.

4. A match (at last). But where does the item writer get off asking for three repair jobs? Why not only one? Or ten? I dunno. The item writer may have asked for three because with three he or she could sample the range of amplifiers and troubles that learners will be expected to handle in the immediate future.

5. Not adequate. Talking a good job isn't the same as doing a good job.

Is the item suitable?

YES   NO   CAN'T

TELL

D. *Objective:* Given a set of diagrams or slides of correctly angled periodontal probe calibrations, write the correct probe reading of each, rounded to the next highest millimeter.*

Criterion Items:

1. On a periodontal probe, which marks are missing?   ✓

2. Look at the slides in Envelope D, and write down the probe reading shown in each. Round your answer to the next highest millimeter.   ✓

3. In Envelope E are slides showing probes that have been inserted into the sulcus. For each slide, tell whether any precautions have been over-looked, and if so, which ones.   ✓

*Objective and criterion items courtesy of Pipe & Associates

D.

1. Not adequate. Even though you may not know what a periodontal probe is, you can see that telling which marks are missing is not the same as writing correct probe readings. (If a dentist could peer through a periodontal probe, would that make it a perioscope? No . . . Don't throw it!)

2. Suitable. Both item and objective ask learners to write correct probe readings. What's that you say? You don't know that the slides in the envelope show correctly handled insertions? Ahh, you are getting to be the sly one. You are correct, of course; we have to assume that the slides represent the objective conditions to call it a match.

3. No again. Describing precautions is not the same as writing correct probe readings.

How'd You Do?

How is your skill at recognizing items relevant to objectives? Are you as good at it as some, better than most? By now you know my answer to this question is that it doesn't matter. What matters is whether you can or cannot perform the skill with adequacy. What's adequate? Well, if I were to have to decide whether you had met my criterion of success, I would do so on this basis:

At least 8 of 10 items correct from Section I, including items 1, 3, 5, 7, 8, and 10,

and

at least 15 of 17 items correct from Section II, including items A3 or A4, B1, C4, and D2.

A final word about the matching of test items to objectives:

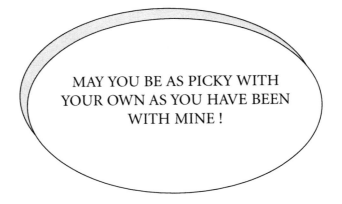

MAY YOU BE AS PICKY WITH YOUR OWN AS YOU HAVE BEEN WITH MINE !

Useful References

1. Mager, R.F. *How to Turn Learners On . . . without turning them off*, Third Edition, 1997.

2. Mager, R.F. *Goal Analysis*, Third Edition, 1997.

3. Mager, R.F. *Preparing Instructional Objectives*, Third Edition, 1997.

4. Schrock, Sharon A., and Coscarelli, William C. C. *Criterion-Referenced Test Development*, 1996. ISBN: 0-9616690-22-0.

Trial
Summary

   Trial was held on January 17, 1984, in Superior Court of World Opinion, Judge Kang A. Roo presiding. After all were seated and the gavel banging had subsided, the judge turned to the plaintiff, Robert F. Mager, and asked that the charges be summarized.
   "They're all guilty, your honor," he said.
   "Yes, yes, I know," replied the judge impatiently. "But I think we should at least identify the defendants and read the charges before we pass sentence. In the interests of justice, that is. Read the charges."
   "Oh, all right," grumbled Mager. "But they're all guilty of tampering with the subject manuscript or its packaging in one way or another.
   "The usual meliorists helped with the initial continuity check, making sure there was some sort of coherence or flow from start to finish. They insisted on wholesale changes of the first draft, leading to a lot of work. They are David Cram and John Warriner."
   "Scoundrels," said the judge. "We'll deal with them later."
   "Those who badgered me on aspects of technical consistency, leading to additional anguished effort, are Bill Deterline, Peter Pipe, Maryjane Rees, and Paul Whitmore."
   "A devious sounding lot," snorted the judge.
   "A whole basketful of people tested for content to make sure the desired outcome was

achieved. They are Norman Carter, Ray Dargus, Margo Hicks, Jane Kilkenny, Dan McCampbell, Tim Mossteller, Dick Niedrich, Peter Selby, Nancy Selden, Andy Stevens, and Eileen Mager."

"Incredible," eyebrowed the judge.

"A number of souls checked to make sure there were no unnecessary turnoffs. These attitude checkers demanded changes to things that slowed them down, turned them off, or rubbed them the wrong way. They are Dale Ball, Tom Frankum, Don DeLong, and Pam Varga."

"You have my complete sympathy," sighed the judge. "Is there more?"

"Yes, your honor," replied Mager. "There are the jargon checkers who pointed to words that were longer or more obscure than necessary, the ones who carried out my poor man's readability test: Joanne Lackey and Katia Prozinski."

"Such impudence will not go unvarnished. Carry on."

"There is a clump of folks who did the title check, poking and picking at words, inferences, and implications. They are Max Forster, Mary Hurley, Dick Lewis, Jeanne Mager, Laura Newmark, Charles Selden, Bill Shanner, Jim Shearer, Charlie Spears, Hal Chitwood, Carol Valen, Casey Williamson, Eileen Mager, Robert Lowe, Linda Marsh, Bill Valen, Stuart Burnett, Susan Klein, Herb Goodyear, JoAnn Egenes, Sally Livingston, Bruce Fredrickson, and Laura Mandel. They are particularly guilty."

"Oh? Why izzat?" queried the judge.

"Because they didn't like MY title and made me give it up."

"Never mind. Justice will triumph."

"Then, your honor, there are those who hooted and hollered and stomped all over the cover designs, trying to make sure that something agreeable to folks other than myself would be used. They are Marshall Arky, Pete Burt, Jim

Edwards, John Feldhusen, Ollie Holt, Roger
Kaufman, Kathy Keeler, Brad Mager, Sue Markle,
Rosalind Kuhl, Harry Shoemaker, Miriam Sierra-
Franco, Randy Mager, Bob Snyder, Wanda Sterner,
Barbara Wachner, John Welser, Dee Williams, C.
Glenn Valentine, and Lori Vanderschmidt. Those
who tested the second edition cover designs
were Johan Adriaanse, Gérard Conesa, Paul Guer-
sch, David Heath, Eileen Mager, Clair Miller,
Fahad Omair, Dan Piskorik, Phil Postel, Jim
Reed, Ethel Robinson, Bill and Carol Valen, Bob
White, and Letitia Wiley."

"There can't be more," incredulated the pon-
tiff.

"Oh, yes. There are those who hooted and
hollered at boo-boos they found in this third
edition: David Cram, Carl Winkelbauer,
Albro Wilson, Eileen Mager, Verne Niner,
Seth Leibler, and Paul Whitmore."

"Well," exclaimed the keeper of the scales.
"I never! What I mean is—I never! Whatever
shall we do with them?"

"Why, we should expose them for what they
are," replied Mager while fervently waggling a
straightened finger. "We should place them in
the pillory of public perception. We should
place their names in posterity where all will
be reminded of their deeds, where all will be
required to note just who was responsible for
the shaping of the innards and the outards of
subject manuscript. The world should know how
helpful they were and that their help was
appreciated."

"So ordered," gaveled the judge. "And let
this be a lesson to everyone. Court's
adjourned."

And it was, too.

Index

Abstractions, defined, 20
Abstract states, objectives that describe, 110
Accomplishments, means of measuring, 3–4
"Affective"objectives, 109–110, 159
Approximations, 90–95
   performance matching and, 92
   small, 93
Assumptions. *See* Approximations

Behavior samples, multiple, 52
Behaviors, sampling, 7

Certification standards, 108
Cheating, avoiding, 5
Clarity
   of main intent, 24-25
   of objectives, 6, 18
   in objective writing, 4-5
Communication, barriers to, 7
Competency. *See also* Performance
   grading on, 109
   judging, 11–12, 14

Condition matching, 77–98, 113-114, 119. *See also* Approximations
   impracticality in, 90–95
   practice items for, 82–89
   process of, 81
   rule for, 81
Conditions defined, 80
   improbable, 103–104
   inferential leaps and, 94–95
   matching to objective, 137
   matching to performance, 137, 141, 157
   range of, 99–102
   stressful, 91
   time range for, 103–104
Consequences of errors, 96
   of grading, 108
Constructing, versus drawing, 129
Covert main intent, 38, 39
Covert performances, 30–32
   identifying, 31–32, 38–40
Criteria, stating in test items, 81
Criterion-referenced evaluation, 10
   versus norm-referenced evaluation, 11–12
Criterion-referenced grading, 106